The Most Interesting People in Sports: 250 Anecdotes

David Bruce

Published by David Bruce, 2023.

While every precaution has been taken in the preparation of this book, the publisher assumes no responsibility for errors or omissions, or for damages resulting from the use of the information contained herein.

THE MOST INTERESTING PEOPLE IN SPORTS: 250 ANECDOTES

First edition. November 25, 2023.

Copyright © 2023 David Bruce.

ISBN: 979-8223777465

Written by David Bruce.

Cover Photograph for *The Most Interesting People in Sports*:
Victoria Borodinova

https://pixabay.com/photos/street-fashion-model-woman-5718052/

https://www.instagram.com/victoriaborodinova/

***

This is a short, quick, and easy read.

Anecdotes are usually short humorous stories. Sometimes they are thought-provoking or informative, not amusing.

***

Do you know a language other than English? If you do, I give you permission to translate this book, copyright your translation, publish or self-publish it, and keep all the royalties for yourself. (Do give me credit, of course, for the original book.)

Chapter 1: From Activism to Coaches

Activism

• At the 1968 Mexico City Olympic Games, Tommie Smith and John Carlos made a memorable political protest against USAmerican racism. After finishing first and third in the 200-meter race, they stood on the winners podium, received their medals, and then each man raised a black-gloved fist in the air. Later, at a news conference, Mr. Carlos stated, "We want to make it clear that white people seem to think black people are animals doing a job. We want people to understand that we are not animals or rats." They paid a heavy price for their protest. They were expelled from the rest of the Olympics, and some people even sent cow manure and dead animals to Mr. Smith's mother. Mr. Smith thinks the stress contributed to her death two years after the Olympics. He also notes that following the protest people treated him as if he had committed murder. Today, both men are respected.[1]

• When Billie Jean King won the women's singles title at Wimbledon in 1966, she was astonished by her prize: a gift certificate for clothing. In Rome, when she won the women's championship at the Open Tennis Tournament in 1970, she received $600, but the winner of the men's championship received $7,500. When she won the women's championship at the U.S. Open in 1972, she received $10,000, but the winner of the men's championship received $25,000. She responded to such inequality in earnings by becoming active in the women's rights movement and fighting for equal rights and for equal pay for all women, including women athletes. In 1973, she founded the Women's Tennis Association. In 1974, she founded both World Team Tennis and the Women's Sports Foundation. Her career earnings reached nearly $2 million, and her outspokenness and popularity helped create the first successful professional tour for women tennis players.[2]

• Hazel Wolf, born 1898, brought girls' basketball to her grade school. She met with the principal and told him that she wanted to play basketball. He replied that girls didn't play that sport, and she responded, "That's because we don't have any basketballs." The principal got her the basketballs.[3]

Actors

• Vince McMahon, Jr., the mastermind of the World Wrestling Federation (WWF), disliked having his wrestling matches regulated by state athletic commissions — and he disliked having to pay money to have the matches regulated. In 1989, Mr. McMahon told New York politicians that pro wrestling is not a sport and therefore it doesn't need to be regulated. He pointed out that the winners and losers are chosen before the matches are held, and he testified that the wrestlers don't want to hurt each other. He told the politicians, "We're storytellers. This is a soap opera performed by the greatest actors and athletes in the world." Following Mr. McMahon's testimony, pro wrestling increased in popularity.[4]

• Gorgeous George was a professional wrestler at night, and he worked at a shipyard during the day. In a wrestling match, he broke his leg, but he didn't go to a doctor. Instead, he went home, and the next morning he went to work as usual. At work, he faked a fall from a ladder — his employer paid his medical bills because he thought that Gorgeous George had broken his leg on the job.[5]

Advice

• At the 1995 British Open, Peter Jacobsen was paired with a 19-year-old Tiger Woods and Ernie Els. Even then, Tiger was very, very good, although Mr. Jacobsen noticed that he was hitting his ball higher in the air than it should be hit at St. Andrews. After they had played together, Tiger asked Mr. Jacobsen, "Is there anything you saw in my game out there that I could improve upon?" Mr. Jacobsen gave him some information about how playing at St. Andrews is different from playing on a USAmerican course, and Tiger thanked him. Later,

Mr. Jacobsen ran into Mr. Els, who told him, "Hey, Peter. Guess what happened? Tiger just walked up to me and asked me if I'd noticed anything in his game that he might improve." Both Mr. Jacobsen and Mr. Els were mightily impressed by Mr. Woods' willingness to ask for advice and by his eagerness to improve his game.[6]

• Tommy Bolt was a great golfer, but his temper sometimes got the best of him on the golf course. During one game, Mr. Bolt played so poorly that he kept throwing his golf clubs in anger. Coming to a par three of 135 yards, Mr. Bolt asked his caddie for advice, and the caddy recommended that he use his two iron. Mr. Bolt said incredulously, "That's crazy! It's only 135 yards." The caddie replied, "But, Mr. Bolt, it's the only club we have left."[7]

Alcohol

• In the 1908 Olympic Games in London, Italian Dorando Pietri appeared to win the gold medal in the marathon, despite being near collapse at the end of the race. In fact, some people say that he fell at least five times before crossing the finish line. And when he did cross the finish line, he was in the arms of an Olympic official. The USAmerican runner, Johnny Hayes, seemed to finish second. However, USAmerican officials lodged an official complaint that Mr. Pietri had received illegal help in crossing the finish line. As a result of the complaint, Mr. Hayes was awarded the gold medal. Mr. Pietri became famous as a result of the race, and he gathered much international sympathy as a result of being stripped of his gold medal. By the way, do you know why Mr. Pietri was staggering as he neared the finish line? According to eyewitness Joe Deakin, who won a gold medal as a relay runner in the 1908 Olympic Games, "The problem was that people along the roadway were giving him glasses of Chantilly instead of water. Pietri wasn't exhausted. He was drunk."[8]

Animals

• Princess, the pet dog of the family of Olympic gold medalist gymnast Bart Conner, was severely arthritic, yet she accompanied

Bart's mother on a three-mile walk every day. The vet told Bart's mother, "Lady, you've just got a motivated dog." She replied, thinking of her three successful sons, "I've got motivated *everything*." By the way, while walking around Los Angeles before the 1984 Olympics, Bart Conner and some other USAmerican gymnasts were recognized by an old wino who asked them for tickets. (Of course, the wino didn't get them.)[9]

• While Scott Hamilton, the 1984 Olympic gold medal winner in men's figure skating, was growing up, he and his family owned several cats in succession, each of which was named Puffy Buttons.[10]

Autographs

• A new generation always comes along that is unknowing of some of the great people of previous generations. Walter Payton once signed an autograph for a young kid who was excited to get his autograph. Just then, Stan Musial arrived, and the young kid's father was excited and asked Mr. Musial to sign an autograph for his son. Mr. Musial did so, but after he left, the young boy asked, "Who was that?" The father replied, "Son, that was Stan the Man." The son asked, "Who?" The father replied, "Stan Musial, the greatest baseball player who ever lived." The son said, "Never heard of him." Joe Kane was present and told his friend Mr. Payton, "Walter, remember this day. Someday you will be forgotten as well. That's the way it works." Apparently, Mr. Payton learned the lesson. He was never accused of being proud, and he realized that all records, including his own, were made to be broken.[11]

• Professional golfer Peter Jacobsen is shocked by the sloppiness of some of the signatures given today by other professional golfers. He was taught to give a legible signature by none other than Arnold Palmer. When Mr. Jacobsen was autographing whatever fans wanted autographed, Mr. Palmer showed Mr. Jacobsen a hat with a scrawl on it and asked, "What the h*ll is that?" Mr. Jacobsen looked and then said, "Uh, that's my autograph." Mr. Palmer then said, "Well, I can't read it, and if I can't read it, these people can't read it. Why in the h*ll would they want your name on a hat if they get home and can't read it? Sign the d*mn thing so they can read it." Ever since then, Mr. Jacobsen has tried to do exactly that.[12]

• NBA great Patrick Ewing studied fine arts at Georgetown University. One of his works of art was stolen from an exhibition, but he suspects that it was stolen so that someone could have his autograph. Mr. Ewing did have a reputation for not giving his autograph because he disliked being the only member of the team who was asked for his autograph. When people asked him for his autograph, he told them, "I'll sign after you've asked my teammates." Also, instead of giving fans his autograph, he often would shake hands with them instead. He reasoned, "It means a lot more than having me sign my name."[13]

• A young fan asked Vanderbilt football great Roy Huggins for an autograph, which he graciously gave. Mr. Huggins then handed the autograph book to another member of the Vanderbilt team, saying, "You want this fellow's autograph, too." The young fan asked who the other player was, and Mr. Huggins told him, "He's a freshman — in two or three years, he'll be All-America." The young fan grabbed the autograph book out of the future All-America player's hand, saying, "I'll wait."[14]

• In 1927, when Bob Feller was nine years old, his father took him to an exhibition game featuring Babe Ruth and Lou Gehrig as well as other stars. Bob wanted a baseball signed by Mr. Ruth and Mr. Gehrig, but the price was $5 — a lot of money at the time. Bob was able to get the $5 by catching gophers. For each gopher, the county treasurer paid a bounty of 10 cents. Bob caught 50 gophers, and he got the autographed baseball.[15]

Automobiles

• Kids learn early about status symbols. Jaimee Eggleton performs as Aladdin in Disney on Ice, but one of his favorite cars, a 1980 Toyota Celica Supra, has over 225,000 miles on it — and runs great. Once a young fan saw Mr. Eggleton driving the car and exclaimed, "That's

Aladdin — and he drives *that*?" Unfortunately, sports careers usually don't last long. On Mr. Eggleton's 30th birthday, his fellow skaters recited funeral chants and picked out a tombstone for him.[16]

• In 1990, tennis player Monica Seles defeated Steffi Graf to win the French Open. To motivate herself to win tournaments, the teenaged Monica often promised herself a reward, such as a new stuffed animal or a new piece of clothing. But this time she had promised herself a brand-new, bright yellow, very expensive sports car — a Lamborghini. However, her parents vetoed this idea on the grounds that a 16-year-old was too young to have a $130,000 automobile.[17]

• Baseball player Satchel Paige liked to drive his green Packard convertible fast. Once he was stopped for speeding, and the judge fined him $40. Mr. Paige took $80 out of his wallet and handed the money to the judge, saying, "Here you go, judge, because I'm coming back this way tomorrow."[18]

Baseball

• In a Dodger baseball game, two men were on base — 1st and 3rd — with two outs. The ball was hit to Dodger third baseman Mickey Hatcher, who had easy outs at 2nd and 1st, but who chose to throw to home, which was the hardest out to make. Waiting for the ball was catcher Joe Ferguson, who made the out. Manager Tommy Lasorda was incredulous. He asked Mr. Hatcher why he had thrown to home plate. Mr. Hatcher explained that he had lost count and thought there was only one out. Mr. Lasorda then turned to Mr. Ferguson and told him, "That was a dumb play, but you were dumber because you were ready for it." Mr. Ferguson had a ready answer: "When you play with dumb players, you gotta think dumb."[19]

• James "Cool Papa" Bell was a Negro Leagues base runner renowned for his speed. According to pitcher Satchel Paige, Cool Papa was so fast that he could flip a light switch off and be in bed before the light went out. This actually has a basis — kind of — in fact. When Satchel and Cool Papa were rooming together, Cool Papa discovered that the light switch in their room was faulty — when switched on or off, it took a little more time than usual to make the connection. When Satchel returned to their room late one night, Cool Papa told him, "You know, Satchel, I'm so fast that I can beat the light!" He then flipped the light switch off and was in bed before the light went out.[20]

• In 1951, manager Leo Durocher's New York Giants came from way behind — on August 1, they were behind by 13½ games — to catch up to the Brooklyn Dodgers and force a playoff game to decide who won the pennant. In the bottom of the ninth, the Giants had one out and men on second and third base. They were also behind 4-2. Bobby Thomson got ready to bat, and Mr. Durocher spoke to him. Mr. Thomson then hit a home run — "The Shot Heard Round the World" — that sent the Giants to the World Series. What did Mr. Durocher say to him? Just this: "If you ever hit one, hit it now."[21]

• The Moscow Red Devils are one of the first baseball teams to be formed in Russia. In fact, baseball is so unknown in Russia that at the Moscow Airport, when the Red Devils were coming to the United States to play exhibition matches, a customs inspector wondered about the purpose of the wooden stick right fielder Andrei Tzelikovsky was carrying. Mr. Tzelikovsky explained that it was a baseball bat, and it was used to play an American sport. The customs inspector then asked, "How far are you supposed to throw it?"[22]

Celebrities

• Groucho Marx once got so angry because of his golf game that he hurled his putter into the green. His country club considered throwing him out, but it relented when he defended himself by saying, "If you throw me out, you'll be sorry. If I'm not a member, I won't have to play golf. And if I don't have to play golf, it'll be a pleasure — not a punishment. You want to make me happy for what I did?"[23]

• The world has an appetite for trivia about its celebrities. For example, when Olga Korbut became a major star at the 1972 Olympics Games in Munich, fans were very interested to learn that she sometimes ate an entire bottle of ketchup at one meal. They were also interested when she said, "Life is marvelous now because I have a tape recorder."[24]

Children

• Chipper Jones' real name is Larry Wayne Jones, Jr., but because of how much he resembled his father, everyone said that he was a chip off the old block and so he soon acquired his nickname. His father was a baseball coach at Pierson Taylor High School in Florida, and he got Chipper started early as a player. While Chipper was too young to swing a real bat, his father cut off a piece of PVC pipe for him to use to hit tennis balls. Chipper rapidly became a confident athlete in more sports than baseball. As a seventh-grade basketball player, he once was fouled and awarded two free throws in a game in which his team was behind by one point with three seconds left to play. The crowd was hostile, and it yelled at him. He waved to the hostile fans, encouraging them to yell louder, and then he made the two free throws to win the game. Of course, he became famous as a player for the Atlanta Braves, and once, while he and his wife were watching football on TV at home 20 young girls came into his yard and started chanting, "Chipper, we love you."[25]

• When he was a kid, NFA quarterback Jim Kelly and his five brothers used to put on helmets and play football in the living room with the couch serving as the end zone. As you would expect, the family furniture paid a heavy price for these indoor games. Their mother once said, "I always said I wouldn't trade my boys for anything, but there were days I would have gladly given them away." Even as a kid, Jim knew he wanted to play in the NFL. At age 11, he got to meet his hero — Pittsburgh Steelers quarterback Terry Bradshaw — and told him, "I'm going to take your job away, Mr. Bradshaw." By the way, when Mr. Kelly attended the University of Miami his freshman year, he ran into problems getting his favorite number. At first, he wanted the number 11 because that was his number in high school. That number was already taken, so then he wanted Terry Bradshaw's number: 12. That number was also already taken. Finally, Mr. Kelly settled for number 7 because that was the only number left on a jersey that fit him.[26]

• Of course, kids will be kids, even when they are elite athletes. In Romania, Nadia Comaneci and some other gymnasts did not turn their lights out when they were supposed to — they waited until they heard Bela Karolyi, their coach, coming to check up on them and then they turned out the lights. They didn't fool Bela, however, and he told them, "Your light was on. You must not be sleepy. Maybe you need to get a bit more tired before you close your eyes." He made them run for a while outside before he let them go to bed again. The next day the young gymnasts were very tired, and after that they turned out their lights when they were supposed to.[27]

• In a T-ball (a version of baseball for very young players) game, an umpire named Laura Benson called a runner out, but the fielder, Tanner Munsey, told her that he had missed the tag, and so Ms. Benson reversed her call. In a game two weeks later, once again Ms. Benson was the umpire and Tanner Munsey was a player. Ms. Benson called a runner safe, but after seeing the disappointed look on Tanner's face, she asked him if he had tagged the runner out. He said he had, and so Ms. Benson reversed her call. Later, Ms. Benson said to the opposing coach, "If a kid is that honest, I have to give it to him."[28]

• MLB star Albert Belle and his twin brother, Terry, were competitive when they were young. One of the things they competed in was reading. Both of them devoured autobiographies, and both of them tried to read more pages than the other. Terry remembers that "if I got up in the middle of the night to go to the bathroom or something, I'd check to see what page [his] marker was on. If it was page 207, then I'd read to page 227 so that when he woke up the next morning, I'd be ahead of him."[29]

• As a child, Scott Hamilton was a very active child. Once, his father, Ernie, was up on the roof working. Suddenly, two-year-old Scott was up on the roof, walking along the edge after climbing up the ladder. On a different occasion, his mother, Dorothy, heard giggling coming from a cabinet above the refrigerator. Even before she opened the cabinet, she knew that she would find Scott. Scott grew up to become the 1984 Olympic gold medalist in men's figure skating.[30]

• As a little girl growing up in Yugoslavia, Monica Seles learned to play tennis on a court made by stretching a string between two parked cars. After she began to win tournaments, Yugoslavians called her the "champion from the parking lots." She was so talented at tennis that she once won a 12-and-under tournament even though she didn't yet know how to keep score and someone had to tell her when her matches were over.[31]

• As very young gymnasts, Dominique Moceanu, Shelly Cavaliere, and Becky Wildgen hung out together. They did not like one coach in particular, so Dominique, whose parents had emigrated from Romania, taught them some Romanian words to say to the coach. The coach had no idea what they were saying, and neither did the two non-Romanian-speaking gymnasts, but Shelly guesses that they were "bad words."[32]

• Young gymnasts tend to look out for each other. At a gymnastics dormitory in the late 1970s, some young gymnasts would sneak away on Saturday afternoons to go to a Burger King for junk food favorites such as a double cheeseburger, fries, and shake. Young gymnast Jackie Cassello said, "If a dorm parent notices that a couple of kids are missing, we'll stick up for them. We'll say they're in the bathroom."[33]

• Lois Lowry, the author of such children's books as *Anastasia Krupnik* and *Number the Stars*, once lost on the television quiz show *Jeopardy*. Her son watched as she missed a question that would have won the game. Afterward, she used to catch him looking at her and shaking his head, shocked that she was so ignorant about baseball.[34]

• As a youngster, soccer superstar Julie Foudy was a tomboy. In a kindergarten play, she won the role of Miss Muffet. Her teacher asked her mother to be sure that little Julie wore a dress to school on the day of the play, but Julie fought against that idea so hard that she got her wish and played the role of Miss Muffet in blue jeans.[35]

• When Mike Tyson was a child, he was small, looked weak, and collected pigeons. One day, a bully killed one of his pigeons in front of him, and instead of running away, as he usually did when he was confronted, he was so angry that he hit the bully. This is how he discovered that he was good at fighting.[36]

• Claude "Butch" Harmon, Jr., had quite a temper when he played golf as a youngster, but his father cured him of it. Whenever Butch got angry on a golf course, his father used to take his golf clubs and lock them up in the trunk of his car for a month before letting Butch play again.[37]

Christmas

• Boston Celtics great Larry Bird, winner of three NBA Championships, grew up impoverished. At one time, his mother worked two jobs to bring home $100 per week; unfortunately, it took $125 to keep the family fed. When Mr. Bird made it to the NBA and the big bucks, he bought his mother a house and filled it with new furniture. As you may expect, a basketball is the first gift that Larry remembers receiving. It was a Christmas gift, and unfortunately, he left it behind a wood-burning stove one night. The next morning, the basketball was bumpy as a result of the excessive heat. Larry played with it anyway. In high school, Larry played basketball wearing a jersey with the number 33, a number that had been worn by his older brother Mike. Larry continued to wear the number 33, and that number has been retired by Larry's high school (Springs Valley High School), by his college (Indiana State), and by the Celtics.[38]

Clothing

• Lots of queens exist in the world: fair queens, prom queens, and rodeo queens. Of course, a rodeo queen is not likely to ride in a chariot powered by four horses. Instead, she is going to be riding the horse, moving like the wind, wearing cowboy boots, and not letting her hat touch the ground. Tina Johnson, a former queen's court advisor for the Yoncalla (Oregon) Rodeo, and therefore an expert, says, "If your hat hits the ground, then your head had better be in it. Losing your hat is a major rodeo queen *faux pas*." (As everyone knows, lots of queens speak French.) So how does a rodeo queen keep her hat on while galloping on a horse? The use of lots of bobby pins helps, as does wearing a hat one size too small. Another expert, the 2007 Yoncalla Rodeo Queen and 2008 Senior Princess Whitney Richey says, "One of the new girls was complaining because her hat was too tight. We told her, 'Take an Advil.'"[39]

• Canadian figure skater Toller Cranston once lived in a house located in a very bad part of Toronto. On the street outside his house could be seen pimps, prostitutes, drug addicts, and hustlers. Once, Mr. Cranston made the mistake of hiring someone to clean out his basement for him. Unfortunately, the cleaner did not know what was valuable and what was not valuable, so he threw out boxes of very expensive skating costumes onto the sidewalk outside Mr. Cranston's house. When Mr. Cranston came home, he saw a riot of activity on the street. The street people had discovered the glittery, jewel-studded costumes, and they were having a grand time putting them on and parading around. For months afterward, Mr. Cranston saw bits and pieces of his costumes being worn by prostitutes getting into customers' cars.[40]

• For a while in her career as a jockey, Julie Krone was racing for several hours a day. Waking up at dawn, she worked horses in the morning, raced at Monmouth Park in New York in the afternoon, and then raced at Atlantic City in New Jersey in the evening. At night, when she went to bed, she tucked her socks and pant legs into her boots, so she could dress more quickly and save time.[41]

• Back when women jockeys first started racing, they tended to upset some of the men jockeys. Sometimes, the men jockeys would be naked in the steam bath and when they would walk — still naked — into the jockeys' room, they would see women jockeys waiting to weigh in. This really didn't bother the women jockeys, one of whom said, "I never notice faces."[42]

• After winning a team gold medal in the 1996 Olympic Games, some members of the United States women's gymnastics team were able to visit the locker room of the Houston Rockets. Dominique Moceanu, who was 4-foot-6, even tried on the jersey of 6-foot-11 Hakeem Olajuwon. The jersey went down to her ankles, so she said, "Nice dress."[43]

• At the 1984 Olympic Games in Los Angeles, USAmerican gymnast Mary Lou Retton took home several souvenirs, including five medals and the leotard she competed in. She told reporters, "I am *never* going to wash this uniform!"[44]

Coaches

• In 1976, the University of Missouri defeated Ohio State's football team, 22-21. One thing that helped Missouri was that a referee called holding on an Ohio State defender, a penalty that set up a score for Missouri. Ohio State coach Woody Hayes furiously argued with the referees about the penalty, but lost the argument. After the game, he walked away with his head down. But the next day, he called Missouri coach Al Onofrio to say that he had watched the film of the game and that the referee's call had been absolutely right. He also apologized for not previously giving the Missouri team the credit it deserved. Coach Onofrio says, "That was his way of congratulating us, even if it was a day later."[45]

• The coaches of teenage athletes sometimes have odd duties. Sarah Hughes was famous enough as a young figure skater to have lots of people notice when she went through a "gawky" phase as she transformed from a child to a young woman. Her coach, Robin Wagner, knew that if Sarah looked at some figure-skating fan websites, she would read that she was "gawky, awkward, had poor posture, lack of maturity." However, Ms. Wagner realized, "At 12 or 13 you're supposed to be gawky and awkward. It's perfectly natural." Therefore, Ms. Wagner did her best to keep Sarah from reading any hurtful comments.[46]

• When Cal Ripken, Jr., was growing up, he was usually able to go to his father — Cal Ripken, Sr., a minor-league and major-league baseball coach — for coaching. However, when his father was busy at work, he was able to go to another person for coaching — Violet Ripken, his mother, who knew much about baseball from being around it constantly. When Cal, Jr., was 11 years old, he pitched a Little League game in 30-degree weather with winds that were so strong that they blew him off the pitcher's mound. Only one person was in the stands — his mother.[47]

• Ohio State University football coach Woody Hayes felt that he and the rest of the coaching staff should shower with the players as a way to show camaraderie. Player Calvin Murray remembers that Woody couldn't reach his back, so someone else would have to wash his back for him. When Woody entered the showers, lots of players would immediately leave, so a big linebacker rinsing the soap from his hair and thus unaware of Woody's entrance would end up washing Woody's back for him.[48]

• In 1952, fumbles resulted in an Oklahoma loss to Notre Dame. All during the first half, the Sooners just couldn't hold onto the football. At halftime, the Sooners waited for the band to get off the field. An Oklahoma majorette threw a baton, and when it came, she dropped it. A fan witnessed the fumble and told Coach Bud Wilkinson, "I see you coach the band, too."[49]

• In 1991, Jerry Glanville coached the Atlanta Falcons. He was eccentric, and he insisted on leaving free tickets at the ticket office for people who never showed up to use them: Elvis Presley, Buddy Holly, and James Dean. Once, he even ordered that a free ticket be made available for the Phantom in *The Phantom of the Opera*.[50]

Chapter 2: From Competition to Food

Competition

- Politics sometimes intrudes on sports in odd ways. In 1937, several Negro Leagues stars, including Satchel Paige and Josh Gibson, played on a team for Dominican Republic dictator Rafael Trujillo, who wanted them to win the championship because he thought that it would boost his popularity. Before the game that determined the championship, team manager Lazaro Salazar informed his players that if they did not win the game, they could end up losing more than a game and a championship — they could very well lose their lives if the dictator decided to have them executed. They won, 6-5.[51]

- The Japanese men were dominant in gymnastics in the 1960s and 1970s, winning several team gold medals in the Olympics and the World Championships. When USAmerican gymnast Kurt Thomas competed against the Japanese at the 1978 World Championships, he knew they were serious about winning. Usually, the Japanese smoked and drank until late, but this time they only smoked. (The semi-abstinence worked — the Japanese won.)[52]

- Triathletes compete in swimming, bicycling, and running in their sport, but it can be difficult to switch from one type of physical activity to the next. Heather Hedrick once competed in a duathlon (bicycling and running). She concentrated so hard on the bicycling that when she first began running, her legs did not even seem to be part of her body. She even asked a fellow competitor, "Where are my legs?"[53]

- For a while, jockey Julie Krone was in a bad slump and failed to finish first in 80 races in a row. In fact, in one race, as she rode toward the finish line knowing that she was going to lose again, she screamed, "I quit! I quit! I quit!" But she didn't quit. She kept racing, she started winning again, and in 1993, she became the first woman to win a Triple Crown race when she won the Belmont Stakes.[54]

• As a young athlete, gymnast Kurt Thomas also competed as a wrestler because the team needed a 98-pounder. Competing as a wrestler was easy for Kurt. Most of the teams he competed against didn't have a 98-pounder, so all he had to do was show up to win.[55]

Conversation

• Soccer superstar Julie Foudy did a lot of work for an anti-smoking campaign, and in April of 1996 she visited the White House, where Donna Shalala, the Secretary of Health and Human Services, gave her a tour. Ms. Shalala stopped outside the Oval Office, where she asked a Secret Service agent if the President was in it. The agent said the President was, so Ms. Shalala said, "We can't show you the room if he's in there. Come on, let's go down to the Cabinet Room." The Secret Service agent was wrong, as Ms. Shalala and Ms. Foudy bumped into President Bill Clinton as he turned the corner. Ms. Foudy said, "We were just looking for you," and they chatted for a while.[56]

• Before the 1991 World Championships in Munich, Germany, figure skaters Kristi Yamaguchi and Kurt Browning trained together. Once, they were traveling together and Mr. Browning asked her, "Do you realize there could be two world champions in this car?" Mr. Browning was right. At the end of the world championships, both Mr. Browning and Ms. Yamaguchi were wearing gold medals.[57]

Curfews

• Babe Ruth partied while he was a major-league baseball player — something that his coaches and managers did not like. Ed Barrow, manager of the Boston Red Sox, sometimes stayed up during road trips so he would know what time his players came in and went to bed. Babe was usually the last one to come back to the hotel. Once, Mr. Barrow asked a porter to let him know when Babe came in. At 6 a.m., the porter woke him and said, "That fellow just came in." Mr. Barrow went to Babe's room. Babe was in bed, but Mr. Barrow pulled back the covers and saw that Babe was fully dressed, including his shoes.[58]

• Green Bay Packers coach Vince Lombardi once set a curfew of 11:30 p.m. for his team. Late one night, he visited a restaurant about four miles away from the Packers' hotel. Unfortunately, his star end, Max McGhee, was also in the restaurant. Mr. Lombardi told Mr. McGhee that he was supposed to be at the hotel, but Mr. McGhee replied, "Not until 11:30 p.m., Coach." Since the time was 11:28 p.m., Mr. Lombardi said, "That gives you exactly two minutes. Do you think you can make it?" Mr. McGhee thought for a moment, and then said, "Not against this head wind, Coach."[59]

Death

• In 1942, the Boston College football team was undefeated near the end of the season but had yet to play an underdog Holy Cross team that had won only four games. In sports, upsets happen, and despite being very heavily favored to win, Boston College went down in defeat, 55-12. Naturally, no Boston College player wanted to attend the party that had been scheduled at the Cocoanut Grove to celebrate an undefeated season. The loss turned out to be a blessing. No Boston College player went to the Cocoanut Grove that night, and the next morning all of the players were alive to read in the newspaper about the fire that had broken out at the Cocoanut Grove, killing more than 400 people.[60]

• Some anecdotes are touching rather than funny, including some anecdotes about death. African-American tennis great Arthur Ashe died of AIDS, which he contracted through a blood transfusion. In an ESPN television interview that discussed the cruel death that lay ahead for Mr. Ashe, interviewer Roy Firestone asked him if he ever wondered, "Why me?" Mr. Ashe replied, "Why not me?" This is exactly the right thing to answer. The AIDS virus doesn't care who you are. It doesn't care about your race, your age, your sex, your religion or lack of it, or your wealth or lack of it. If it can take over your body, it will.[61]

Education

• When Alex Rodriguez went into a slump early in his career, he struck out against Roger Clemens with the bases loaded. On television, Alex cursed and threw his bat. Watching the game and seeing Alex's poor behavior was his old Boys Club coach, Eddie Rodriguez, who telephoned and told him, "Your actions can shame everyone who helped you get this far. You embarrass your family, friends, coaches, and mentors, like Mr. [J.D.] Artega [Sr., a father figure to Alex]. No one can act perfectly all the time. Everyone makes mistakes. But we must always strive to do the right thing. That means playing hard and honorably. In doing so, you honor all those people who supported you throughout your life." Mr. Rodriguez resolved to do his best to "always strive to do the right thing."[62]

• Robert Hill, coach of the Jackson State football team, taught his backs well, and he was flexible when he needed to be. For example, he taught his backs the correct foot to start running on when the football was snapped, but Walter Payton preferred to use his other foot because it felt more comfortable to him. Therefore, Mr. Hill would demonstrate the correct foot to use, and then tell the backs, "OK, everybody, I want you to do it this way." But he then would turn to Mr. Payton and say, "And you, fool, do it your way."[63]

• British long-distance runner Paula Radcliffe attended Sharnbrook upper school in Bedfordshire during 1987-1992. Vaughan Caradice was her maths teacher. One day Mr. Caradice was writing an exam question on the chalkboard when young Paula gently told him, "You might want to have another look at that." Mr. Caradice says, "When Paula says that, you have another look — and she was right: I'd made a mistake."[64]

• Some schools place way too emphasis on the football and other sports teams, and other schools make fun of those schools. Antioch had no sports teams and no mascots. Upset that other schools placed such an emphasis on athletics rather than academics, Antioch students adopted their own mascot: a Brussels sprout.[65]

• Elfi Schlegel missed a lot of school while performing in gymnastics at a young age, but her competing in international gymnastics had an advantage for her class. After Ms. Schlegel returned to her native Canada after competing in another country, she would give a class presentation on that country.[66]

• Even in college, marathon swimmer Diana Nyad was a daredevil. While attending Emory University in Atlanta, Georgia, she jumped from a 4th-floor window while wearing a parachute. Emory University officials "requested" that she attend some other university.[67]

• Muhammad Ali lost his last fight — in a unanimous decision — to Trevor Berbick. When a reporter asked Mr. Berbick if he had learned anything from Mr. Ali during the fight, Mr. Ali answered for Mr. Berbick: "I taught him to retire before he's 40."[68]

Family

• Major-league baseball player Roberto Clemente learned a lot from his parents. During World War II, food was scarce for many families in Puerto Rico, and Roberto remembers, "During the war, when food was hard to get, my parents fed their children first and took what was left. They always thought of us." His father, Melchor, harvested sugarcane — a job with low pay despite the hard work — for a living. Sometimes, they would see Melchor's boss driving a fancy car, and Melchor would say to Roberto, "He is no better than you." When Roberto was nine years old, he wanted a bicycle. Melchor told him, "Earn it." So Roberto got a job in the morning lugging a heavy milkcan back and forth from a neighbor's house and the local general store. After three years of work, he had saved $27, with which he bought a used bicycle.[69]

• The family of golfer Nancy Lopez was very supportive of her. Young Nancy was not allowed to wash dishes because she needed to protect her hands, and so her mother washed the dishes instead. In fact, her mother once decided not to buy a dishwasher so that she could use the money to pay for Nancy to play in tournaments instead. The sacrifice paid off. As an adult Nancy became a superstar golf player, and at age 10 she won a tournament by 110 strokes![70]

• In 1970, Cathy Rigby won the silver medal on the balance beam at the World Games in Ljubljana, Yugoslavia — this was the first medal ever won by a USAmerican woman gymnast in international competition. Ms. Rigby sent this telegram back home to her parents: "Have won second place on the beam — the silver medal for the U.S. and you."[71]

• In 1994, Ukrainian gymnast Svetlana Boguinskaia stayed at the Massachusetts home of David Freedman and his family, where she was a perfect guest. Mr. Freedman says, "My family fell in love with Svetlana. She even let our twin daughters wear her Olympic medals."[72]

Fans

• In the 1999 NFL Draft, the Philadelphia Eagles used their first pick — the second overall — to make quarterback Donovan McNabb a member of the team. Unfortunately, some fans had wanted the Eagles to choose Ricky Williams, a star running back for the University of Texas and the winner of the Heisman Trophy. Mr. McNabb could not believe that he was being booed. He even told his mother, "Mom, they're booing me." Still, he said, "Fans are always going to state their opinion, and I respect them for that. I've learned it doesn't matter what fans say in the beginning, just as long as they're cheering in the end." Fast-forward to 2002, just before the NFC Championship game, which, unfortunately, the Eagles lost to the St. Louis Rams, 29-24. Before the game, Eagles fans reenacted the 1999 NFL Draft. This time, when Mr. McNabb's name was announced as the Eagles' first pick, fans cheered. In 1999, Philadelphia radio personality Angelo Cataldi had led the booing; this time, he helped lead the cheering, saying, "I just thought we needed one final moment of absolution. We gave him a response more worthy of his talents and what he has done. It looks to me like he will be an absolutely terrific quarterback for the next ten years."[73]

• Country comedian Jerry Clower once took his son to see the unveiling of a statue of Stan Musial at a St. Louis Cardinals baseball game. This was a big event, and Mr. Musial and all of the teammates he had had in his rookie season were invited to the unveiling. At one point in the festivities, the players were introduced according to their batting order, and when batter number three was introduced, the crowd went crazy. At first, Mr. Clower thought the crowd would be disappointed because he knew that Mr. Musial batted fourth, but an old-timer in the audience told him, "The Old Hustler is fixing to come out. The fellow is fixing to come out that believed in giving an honest day's work for an honest day's pay. Why, I remember seeing him score from first base once on a bunt." This is no reflection on Mr. Musial, who also hustled and who got his well-deserved applause and standing ovation, but this particular applause and standing ovation were for Enos Slaughter.[74]

• Basketball player John Stockton played point guard at Gonzaga University, a Spokane, Washington, Catholic school whose most famous graduate was Bing Crosby. When the Utah Jazz drafted Mr. Stockton in the first round, he was unknown, and he wondered what the Jazz fans would think. At draft time, Mr. Stockton was in NBA draft headquarters in New York, and he spoke with someone who was on the telephone with a person at the Salt Palace, where Jazz fans had gathered. Mr. Stockton asked, "Are they booing?" The man with the telephone replied, "They're not booing. They're all asking, 'Who?'"[75]

• Hank Aaron felt that for much of his career he did not get the press that other athletes did, but of course that changed when he started to close in on Babe Ruth's career home-run record. Then he began to be surrounded by sports writers, some of whom were flattering but insincere. For example, one sports writer told Mr. Aaron that he had been following his career for 20 years, and then he asked him whether he batted right-handed or left-handed! Of course, some people were true fans, as was the boy who wrote to tell him that the only candy bars he ate were Oh Henry! candy bars.[76]

• Stunt rider Matt Hoffman is a good man on a bicycle. In 2002, even after breaking his wrist, he decided to go to Brazil to take part in a tour throughout South America. He performed a number of tricks, and then he noticed three Brazilian fans wearing shirts with the number "900." Mr. Hoffman had invented the very difficult 900 trick in which he turns two-and-a-half times while in the air. Even though he hadn't performed the trick for seven years, he decided to try to perform it for these three fans. Despite his broken wrist, he performed the 900 trick perfectly.[77]

• Jimmy Carter remembers that back when African-American fighter Joe Louis was defeating white boxers with ease and regularity, black neighbors of the Carters would visit so that they could listen to the fights on the radio. The blacks were always very polite, and they were always very quiet, and they would thank the Carter family for allowing them to listen to the radio. Then they would walk about 100 yards away and enter a house in which lived a black family. At that time the Carters could hear yells of jubilation over Mr. Louis' most recent victory.[78]

• Tommy Lasorda occasionally coached a minor-league team for a few games as a morale-booster and inspiration-booster. Minor-league player Casey Kennedy remembers one game when a ball went down the line. It was a close call, and the umpire called foul. Mr. Lasorda ran out of the dugout and vociferously argued with the umpire for 10 minutes. When he returned to the dugout, Casey asked him, "Was it fair or foul?" Mr. Lasorda replied, "I don't know. I just wanted to give the fans a show."[79]

• Early in his career, Carl Yastrzemski took some abuse from fans because he was taking over for the great hitter Ted Williams. As a rookie, Mr. Williams hit 31 home runs with a .327 batting average. As a rookie, Mr. Yastrzemski hit 11 home runs with a .266 batting average.

In one game, Mr. Yastrzemski even wore cotton in his ears because of the fan abuse. Of course, he soon became a star and took the Red Sox to two World Series, each of which they lost in the seventh game.[80]

• Following sports today is much different from the way people followed sports in the good old days. When Danville, Kentucky's Centre College beat Harvard, 6-0, in an away game in 1921, Centre College fans gathered at the Danville telegraph office and followed the game by telegram. Anita Curry, born 1902, remembered, "They had the street blocked off. And you would wait for the telegram to come down. 'Centre made five yards!' Every play. And we'd shout, 'Woo!'"[81]

• Chicago Bear tackle George Musso was blocked in a game so fiercely that he lost consciousness. Trainer Andy Lotshaw ran over to Mr. Musso just as he was regaining consciousness. Mr. Lotshaw asked, "How are you feeling?" Mr. Musso replied, "OK — but how's the crowd taking it?"[82]

Fathers

• Boston Red Sox player Carl Yastrzemski's father had the chance to play minor-league baseball for the Brooklyn Dodgers, but unfortunately it was during the Great Depression, and so he turned them down so he could continue working on his potato farm and continue being sure that his family could eat. However, he was determined that his son would have a chance to be a professional baseball player and so he did such things as form his own baseball team. Each member of the team was named either Yastrzemski or Skonieczny (the maiden name of Carl's mother) because each member of the team was also related to every other member. Carl's father would also not allow him to play football during his senior year because of fear of an injury. Carl secretly went out for the football team anyway, and when his father found out, he went to the football practice field and dragged Carl — literally — off it. Carl played baseball at the University of Notre Dame, where he once hit a baseball during batting practice over

500 feet onto the football team's practice field. Football coach Hank Stram looked at the ball and said, "I bet Yastrzemski hit this."[83]

• The father of Boston Celtics great Bill Russell didn't want money from his son, even though Bill was making good money as a star for the Boston Celtics. Whenever Bill wanted to give him money, he would say, "I got a job. I got my own d*mn money." Bill would then say, "But that's a terrible job. You work in a foundry. All your pants have holes in them from the sparks. There's dust and metal particles in the air. And you're by furnaces and then you go outside and it's freezing. It's *terrible*." Bill's father would reply, "I can't quit this job." Then he would explain why he couldn't quit: "Listen, son. I've given these people thirty-five of the best years of my life. Now, I'll give them a few of the *bad* ones!" Even though Bill's father never would take money from him, Bill figured out a way to give him a new car. He simply paid for the car and told the dealership where to deliver it. When the brand-new car was delivered, Bill's father cried. A little later, he called Bill to say, "I'm really p*ssed off at you." Bill asked, "Why?" His father explained, "Because I just got the first speeding ticket of my life!"[84]

• When NBA star David Robinson's father, Ambrose, was in high school in Little Rock, Arkansas, he took a college exam. He scored very high on it, higher than most of the white students, but because he was African-American, some people felt that he could have not scored that high. Therefore, he had to take the college entrance test again while test proctors carefully watched him. This time, Ambrose Robinson earned an even higher score! With a father like that, David had to get good grades, of course. In junior high, David's report card for a grading period had one A, two B's, and a C. David's father grounded him for six weeks.[85]

• Basketball great Michael Jordan's father died senselessly. He was murdered for his money when a couple of hoodlums found him sleeping in his car. Mr. Jordan did not attend the trial, and he did not ask for capital punishment for the murderers of his father. When asked about the killers, he would say, "My father is dead. That's all I care about."[86]

• When professional beach volleyball player Gabrielle Reece was five years old, her father, Robert Eduardo Reece, died in an airplane crash. At the time of the accident, he was wearing a silver cross on a necklace. The necklace and silver cross were recovered and given to Gabrielle and are among her most treasured possessions.[87]

Fights

• Eddie Shore was a tough player in the NHL, and he fought often. King Clancy would not run away from a fight, but he would try to find creative ways to avoid fights. During a game pitting Mr. Shore's Boston Bruins against Mr. Clancy's Toronto Maple Leafs, Mr. Clancy knocked Mr. Shore to the boards. Mr. Shore took off his gloves preparatory to fighting Mr. Clancy, but Mr. Clancy grabbed his hand, shook it, and asked how Mr. Shore was doing. Mr. Shore laughed, and no fight took place.[88]

• Joe Louis defeated Max Baer after Mr. Baer was counted out after getting up on one knee. Mr. Baer retained a sense of humor about his loss. When someone asked how he felt about being counted out when he was on one knee, he said, "I could have struggled up once more, but when I get executed, people are going to have to pay more than $25 a seat to watch it."[89]

• Oliver Marcelle played third base in the 1920s. Unfortunately, despite being an outstanding third baseman, he had a hot temper and constantly fought both members of other teams and his own teammates. His career ended because of fighting — he retired after a teammate bit off his nose.[90]

Food

• During the Jim Crow days, black ballplayers often carried food with them while traveling because sometimes they had trouble finding a restaurant to serve them. "Borrowing" was common on the team buses and cars, and so ballplayers would go to great lengths to protect their food. Harry Kincannon, a pitcher, once brought some fried chicken onto the team bus. He ate some of it, then he pulled out a gun and threatened his teammates, saying that if any of them wanted to taste lead all they had to do was to taste his chicken. Mr. Kincannon then fell asleep. One teammate relieved him of the gun and unloaded it, and another teammate relieved him of his fried chicken and passed pieces of it around to other players. After all of the chicken had been eaten, they made a necklace out of the bones and put it around Mr. Kincannon's neck. When Mr. Kincannon woke up, everyone, including Mr. Kincannon, laughed.[91]

• Back in the days when Romania was a Communist country and much of its food was exported, food for its own citizens could be rare, even for people such as Nadia Comaneci, after she retired from gymnastics. She had an old neighbor, around 70 years old, named Aleca Petre, who would get up early at 4 a.m., then stand in line during cold winter weather to get into a grocery store to see what food was on the shelves. According to Nadia, most of the time only beans, mustard, and mayonnaise were on the shelves. However, he would bring her milk when he could — and sometimes even some meat. Nadia points out that Romanians were always willing to share what food they had. She says, "That is the way Romanians are: We share what we have."[92]

• A horse trainer named "Fatty" Anderson was a big eater, and he competed in eating contests. In one contest against a champion eater from Cuba, the two big eaters ate many chickens and many pounds of oysters, and then started in on apple pies. The Cuban eater was beaten, but Mr. Anderson finished eating his most recent apple pie, then took the last remaining piece of pie from the Cuban's plate and signaled for a waiter — he wanted a slice of cheese put on the piece of apple pie.[93]

• In 1963, in the back room of Trader Vic's, a San Francisco restaurant, world champion eater Bozo Miller made big money by eating 27 two-pound chickens. For a while, his competitor kept up, but eventually the competitor stopped eating, remained sitting, and watched Mr. Miller eat his way to a $10,000 purse. To eat that much, Mr. Miller trained hard. For two weeks he stuffed himself to stretch his stomach into competitive shape — and he gained over 25 pounds.[94]

• As a young man, world-class women's gymnastics coach Bela Karolyi found work in a slaughterhouse in his native Romania. This job wasn't all bad, since he could hide meat in his pocket at the end of the day and be sure he would eat supper that night.[95]

• In 1973, at the Chunichi Cup, USAmerican gymnast Joan Rice helped satisfy Soviet gymnast Ludmila Tourischeva's sweet tooth (and break training) by using a rope to lower Coca-Colas from her hotel window two stories below to Ludmila's window.[96]

Chapter 3: From Football to Media

Football

• When Donovan McNabb, later a quarterback for the Philadelphia Eagles, was in the seventh grade, he started playing football, first as a running back, then as a quarterback. His parents motivated him to score. His father says, "We told him we'd give him $10 for each touchdown, and if he didn't score, he'd have extra duties in the house. That started getting expensive, so we [reduced the reward amount and] broke out the $5 bills." For his first couple of years at Syracuse University, Mr. McNabb played basketball as well as football, but the amount of time it took to go from in shape for football to in shape for basketball reduced his basketball playing time and he spent a lot of time on the bench. When the Syracuse Orangeman lost to the University of Kentucky in the 1996 NCAA Championship game, Mr. McNabb did not play; however, he led the cheering for his team from the bench. Syracuse basketball coach Jim Boeheim said, "Usually when a guy wants to play and he's good and he's not playing, he's not man enough to still support the team. But there was Donovan, pumping guys up, slapping them on the back, leading the bench guys."[97]

• In 1982, when the Super Bowl pitted Cincinnati against San Francisco, a young church-going woman admitted that she had bet $2 on Cincinnati, and after Mass on Super Bowl Sunday, she asked her priest, Msgr. Vincent Fecher, if that were wrong. He replied, "This is so important, I don't want to decide. But I'll tell you what: I was going back into church for something; why don't I just ask the Lord if it was wrong?" Father Vincent returned in a few moments, and the young woman asked, "What did He say?" Father Vincent replied, "He said yes, it was wrong. You should have bet the $2 on San Francisco." (By the way, San Francisco defeated Cincinnati, 26-21.)[98]

• When Bo Jackson, a professional baseball player for the Kansas City Chiefs, started playing professional football for the Los Angeles

Raiders, people wondered how well he would do. He soon showed them. In his fifth game for the Raiders, he made a 91-yard touchdown, running so hard that he crossed the end zone and ran into a tunnel that led to the locker rooms. When he returned to the end zone, he pretended to swing at the football with an imaginary baseball bat.[99]

• The first football (and soccer ball) was a human head. In the 8th century, the Vikings invaded England and were defeated. The English soldiers decapitated the Viking leader and used his head to play a kicking game. Later, the same game was played with a blown-up cow bladder. Because the cow bladder kept popping, pigskin was used to cover it and give it durability. Today, the inside rubber bag of a football is known as a bladder, and the football is known as a pigskin.[100]

• Ohio sportscaster Jimmy Crum frequently watched Ohio State football coach Woody Hayes during practice. Once a linesman got creamed at the line and Mr. Hayes yelled at him, "How many times do I have to tell you, before you run — think, think, think!" A few minutes later, the same linesman was again creamed at the line. This time Mr. Hayes yelled, "How many times do I have to tell you, don't think — just run, run, run!"[101]

• Lakia Washington was the only girl player on the Groton School football team. The male members of the team supported her, and they always told her not to take off her helmet until after the game — when the other team would discover that one of the people who had been running touchdowns against them was a girl.[102]

Gambling

• Chris Lemmon, the son of Jack Lemmon, once got lucky when a race tout gave him tips that turned out to be four winners in a row. Actor Walter Matthau heard him talk about his winnings, didn't believe him, and said, "I've got a Martian living in my house. His name's Harry, and he's from Mars." Chris protested that he had actually had four winners in a row, and he said that he would share the tout's next tip with him. Walter said, "Harry and I'll be waiting." Eventually, the tout arrived and gave a tip, Chris shared the tip with Walter, both Chris and Walter bet on the recommended horse, and the horse lay down and took a nap when the race started. Walter told Chris, "You know that Martian I told you about, the one living in my house? Well, his relatives moved in."[103]

• After Jim Thorpe retired as a professional athlete, he worked as an extra in movies. Once, he and several other extras participated in a contest to see who could make the longest standing long jump. Betting on the outcome was William Frawley, who later played Fred Mertz in the TV sitcom *I Love Lucy*. Mr. Frawley knew of Mr. Thorpe's athletic prowess, so he bet on the "old" man. Mr. Frawley won his bet, and Mr. Thorpe's jump of 10 feet, 8 inches, was only 6 inches shy of the current world record.[104]

Gifts

• When NFL player Esera Tuaolo decided to come out of the closet, the media took notice. *New York Times* sportswriter Bob Lipsyte wrote a sensitive article. *Real Sports With Bryant Gumbel* on HBO did a very good piece. Mr. Tualo then appeared on *Good Morning America*, and the show was broadcast live on a JumboTron screen in Times Square. The *Good Morning America* studios overlook Times Square, and after the interview Mr. Tualo was a hero on Times Square. Celebrity publicist Howard Bragman, who has helped many athletes and actors come out, says, "Real New Yorkers — the hot dog vendors and cops on the street, no quiche eaters they — hailed Tuaolo as a star and a hero for his courage. They were giving him free hot dogs, free T-shirts — you would never have believed it was New York."[105]

• On June 15, 1988, New York Met Darryl Strawberry hit two home runs against St. Louis as a gift to his son, Darryl Strawberry, Jr., who had turned three years old on that day. Mr. Strawberry had promised his son only one home run, but his excellent hitting doubled the gift. After the game, which the Mets won, Mr. Strawberry said, "This is my kid's birthday, and I promised him I would hit a home run for him. He's always talking about hitting home runs. You can ask his mommy."[106]

Golf

• Groucho Marx once made a hole-in-one while playing golf. Because he was a celebrity, the newspapers made a big deal out of it, and the Boston *Globe* ran a visual aid of three photographs — one of Groucho, and two others of Bobby Jones and Walter Hagen, both big golf stars of the day. Appearing alongside the three photographs was the headline "Groucho joins the immortals." The next day, Groucho played golf again, but this time several members of the media followed him. Because of all the attention, his golf game suffered and Groucho was many, many strokes above par. The next day the Boston *Globe* ran roughly the same visual aid, but a blank space appeared where Groucho's photograph had been. This time the headline was "Groucho leaves the immortals."[107]

• Dow Finsterwald won the 1958 U.S. PGA championship. Once, TV sports journalist Jimmy Crum was golfing with him and remarked that when he saw Mr. Finsterwald make a great shot, he felt like breaking all his clubs and quitting golf. Mr. Finsterwald replied, "Every shot I hit, whether it's on tour or at an exhibition match like this one, is directly related to the kind of clothes my family wears, the kind of food we eat, and the kind of roof we have over our heads. This is my business. Until golf becomes that serious to you, just play to have fun."[108]

• In 1952, Katherine Hepburn and Spencer Tracy starred in *Pat and Mike*, about a woman athlete. The script called for Ms. Hepburn's character to win against several famous women athletes who made cameo appearances in the movie, including golfer Betty Hicks and tennis players Alice Marble and Gussie Moran. However, one part of the script had to be rewritten. Golfer Babe Zaharias was too proud to come in second to Ms. Hepburn's character, and in the movie, Babe wins the tournament by one stroke.[109]

• Jack Lemmon, and Chris, his son, played golf frequently. In one game both Jack and Chris hit their golf balls into a weedy ditch that was surrounded by signs that said, "BEWARE RATTLESNAKES." Neither wanted to brave the rattlesnakes, so they left their golf balls there. Later, they saw a 10-year-old kid carrying all of the "BEWARE RATTLESNAKES" signs — and a bag of golf balls. Jack laughed and said, "There goes a future president."[110]

• Nancy Lopez' parents believed that she could be a good golfer even when she was very young. Her mother even gave up golf herself so that Nancy could have more time on the golf course being trained by her father. They simply couldn't afford to have all three of them play golf. Her father built a floor-to-ceiling trophy case for her. For a long time, it displayed mainly dishes, but today it is not big enough to hold all of her trophies.[111]

• To win the 1938 Cleveland Open, all Ky Laffoon had to do was to make a putt from five feet. However, he missed the putt twice and became so angry that he threw his putter down on top of the ball. The ball flew up into the air and fell into the cup, making Mr. Laffoon the champion.[112]

Good Deeds

• Max Schmeling was a German boxer who became heavyweight champion of the world in 1930. Later, he rescued two Jewish teenagers during the Holocaust. In 1938, David Lewin, Mr. Schmeling's Jewish friend, asked him for help. Mr. Lewin and his family wanted to escape from Berlin. When *Kristallnacht*, a time of violence against Jews, began on November 9, Mr. Lewin asked Mr. Schmeling, who had recently returned from a business trip, to hide his two sons, Heinz and Werner, then fourteen and fifteen years old. Mr. Schmeling kept the two boys in his room at a hotel, and when the violence of *Kristallnacht* lessened a few days later on November 12, he took them to his home. A couple of days after that, he took the boys to their father, and the family was able to escape the Holocaust. This good deed was kept secret for decades until Heinz organized a gala dinner in honor of Mr. Schmeling when the champ was 84 years old. Heinz then told the story of Mr. Schmeling's act of bravery to the guests. He said, "I'm going to tell you what kind of a champion Max Schmeling is. He risked everything for us. If we would have been found in his room, I would not be here this evening and neither would Max." Mr. Schmeling had wanted his good deed kept secret, but Heinz publicly spoke about it because he did not want Mr. Schmeling to die without being recognized for what he had done. (By the way, when boxing champion Joe Louis died while owing money to the Internal Revenue Service, Mr. Schmeling sent money to Mr. Louis' widow.)[113]

• Some boys playing baseball in a park once saw Babe Ruth stopped at a red light, and they requested, "Come on, let us see you hit a few." Babe parked his car and spent 30 minutes hitting easy fly balls so the boys could catch them — and he hit a few that traveled a very long distance. Babe was generous with money, too. One day during spring training, rain resulted in the cancellation of a game, so he went to a racetrack, where he won $9,000. In Babe's day, players were not paid during spring training, so most of his teammates were broke. Babe went back to the clubhouse, threw the $9,000 on top of an equipment trunk, and said, "Well, boys, look what I found." He was also kind to Father Matthias, who ran St. Mary's Industrial School for Boys, where Father Matthias taught him how to play baseball. Babe bought Father Matthias a new Cadillac each year, and when some of the buildings at St. Mary's were destroyed in a fire, he arranged for the band of St. Mary's to tour with the New York Yankees and hold concerts to raise money for new buildings. He also returned occasionally to play baseball with the boys of St. Mary's.[114]

• Boston Celtics great Bob Cousy is a kind man who did much for pro basketball, both on the court and off the court. On the court, he helped the Boston Celtics win championships, and off the court, he spoke at banquets and gave time and tips to kids. Sportswriter Jim

Murray knows how kind Mr. Cousy is. In many years of writing about athletes in a daily column, he received exactly three letters of appreciation from the athletes he wrote about (as of the publication of his 1965 book, *The Best of Jim Murray*). The first letter of appreciation was written by Mr. Cousy.[115]

• In 1984, after Boston Celtics great Larry Bird won his second NBA Championship, he did a notable deed. Equipment manager Walter Randall had been with the Celtics since the 1949-1950 season — the very first NBA season. However, equipment managers don't get championship rings — that is, until Mr. Bird bought one for Mr. Randall. The ring made Mr. Randall, who died of cancer the following season, very happy.[116]

Hitters

• Although Rogers Hornsby was a great hitter, he could be a very unpopular guy. While he was playing for the Giants, he had dinner with Giants shortstop Ed Farrell. When someone stopped at the table and asked him if the Giants had a chance to win the pennant, Mr. Hornsby replied, "Not with Farrell playing shortstop." Later, he played for the Braves. Asked if the Braves had a chance to win the pennant, Mr. Hornsby pointed to the players, and then replied, "These humpty-dumpties?" Finally, when Mr. Hornsby was playing for the St. Louis Browns, and owner Bill Veeck fired him, the Browns players bought a silver trophy for Mr. Veeck and had it inscribed with this message: TO BILL VEECK FOR THE GREATEST PLAY SINCE THE EMANCIPATION PROCLAMATION, JUNE 10, 1952, FROM THE PLAYERS OF THE ST. LOUIS BROWNS."[117]

• Major-league umpire Jocko Conlan had enormous respect for hitter Ted Williams. In Minneapolis, in the last of the ninth inning, Mr. Williams came to bat with two outs and his team down by one run, with the bases loaded. It was an exciting game, and Mr. Conlan ended it by calling a third strike on Mr. Williams. Of course, Mr. Williams' third-base coach, Donie Bush, came running in, screaming that the ball had been thrown at Mr. Williams' ankles and should have been called a ball. At this point, Mr. Williams said, "No, Donie, it was a good pitch. It was a perfect strike, right at the knees. I should have hit it." Mr. Conlan says, "I could have thrown my arms around him. I walked off the field and I thought, 'What a man this is!' I never had anyone else in my career do anything like that."[118]

• Cleveland Indians player Rocky Colavito hit four home runs in four consecutive at-bats in a single game on June 10, 1959, against the Baltimore Orioles. However, the very next year he was traded to the Detroit Tigers. In return for Mr. Colavito, the Indians got Harvey Kuenn, who had batted .353, but who didn't hit as many home runs as Mr. Colavito. Actually, the Indians management didn't want their players to hit too many home runs since management didn't want to pay the big salaries of big home-run hitters. In fact, the year Mr. Colavito hit four home runs in a single game he made management angry at him because he hit 42 home runs that season even though his contract rewarded him if he hit fewer than 40 home runs during the season.[119]

• Charlie Grimm managed the Chicago Cubs to pennants in 1932 and 1935, but they lost the World Series both times. A scout tried to get him interested in a pitcher by saying that he struck out 27 batters in a single game, with a single batter in the ninth inning getting a foul off him. Mr. Grimm replied, "Sign the kid who hit the foul ball. We need hitters more than pitchers."[120]

• In 1983, Cal Ripken, Jr., was hit in the ribs with a pitch thrown by Rich Dotson of the White Sox. Mr. Ripken did not rub the place where the baseball had hit him. Instead, he jogged to first base, and then he yelled at Mr. Dotson, "Is that as hard as you can throw?" And yes, the next time he batted against Mr. Dotson, he hit a double.[121]

• Early in his career, Babe Ruth was a very good pitcher, but he upset some veterans on the Boston Red Sox team when he wanted to take batting practice. One day, he arrived at the ball field to find out that all of his bats had been sawn in half. (Of course, a little later, he earned the veterans' respect.)[122]

• Baseball player Bobby Bonilla was usually even tempered, but in 1988, after striking out with a called third strike, he yelled at the umpire. Later that day, he watched a video replay, and the next day he apologized to the umpire, admitting that the pitch had been a strike and he had been wrong.[123]

• Ty Cobb was an intensely competitive hitter, even late in his career. At age 42, he was ready to bat when his manager asked him to allow a pinch hitter to bat for him. Mr. Cobb replied, "Nobody ever bats for Cobb!" Then, in true Hollywood style, he made a game-winning hit.[124]

Hockey

• On New Year's Day of 1967 at about 8 p.m., only two reporters were working at the *Chicago Sun-Times*. One of them was new-kid Roger Ebert; the other was respected veteran Mike Royko. Mr. Royko came over to see who else was working before the graveyard shift came on, and since a snowstorm was starting, he asked the new kid how he was going to get home. Roger was going to take a train home, so Mr. Royko offered to drive him to the train station. First, however, he had to stop at a 24-hour pharmacy. It was busy, so to kill time, Mr. Royko invited Roger to get a drink at a bar — an eye-opener place. He ordered, "Two blackberry brandies and short beers," and then explained, "Blackberry brandy is good for hangovers. You never get charged for a beer chaser." Roger felt good. He was a reporter, he was having a drink with the great Mike Royko, he was living life as it ought to be lived. On the radio, an announcer was talking about a Blackhawks hockey game. The Blackhawks scored, then they scored again, and then they scored again. Roger said, "The Blackhawks are really hot tonight." Mr. Royko looked at him, and then he said, "Where you from, kid? Downstate?" The answer was yes. Mr. Royko asked, "Ever seen a hockey game?" The answer was no. Mr. Royko then said,

"That's what I thought, you ***hole. Those are the game highlights."[125]

• Not every retired NHL player expects to be voted into the Hockey Hall of Fame. Former New York Rangers player Rod Gilbert, who played — very well, in fact — from 1960 to 1978, did not. When the call announcing his election to the Hall of Fame came in 1982, he was sound asleep, taking a nap, because he figured that no such call would be coming. Judy, his wife, answered the telephone, and then woke up her husband to give him the good news.[126]

Hunting and Fishing

• When Bo Jackson left Auburn University, he had the choice of playing either professional baseball for the Kansas City Chiefs or professional football for the Tampa Bay Buccaneers. When reporters asked Mr. Jackson what he was going to decide, he said that he would choose the sport he loved the most, then he joked, "And what I really love the most is hunting and fishing." Eventually, of course, he chose to play professional baseball for the Chiefs. (Later, he also played professional football for the Los Angeles Raiders.)[127]

• In 1984, Mark Parker of Linden, Louisiana, caught a two-pound bass in Caney Lake. One hour later, he prepared to clean the fish. To do so, he stuck his finger into the bass' mouth — and was bitten by a small water moccasin that the bass had swallowed just before striking Mr. Parker's bait. Mr. Parker spent some time in a hospital, but he survived.[128]

Injuries and Illnesses

• Major-league baseball pitcher Bob Gibson was sickly — and impoverished — as a young kid. He remembers a rat biting him on the ear — this is one of his earliest memories. He suffered through a number of illnesses as a youngster: He had rickets, bronchial asthma, and a rheumatic heart. At age three, he nearly died from pneumonia. His older brother, Leroy, whose nickname was Josh (after Negro Leagues standout hitter Josh Gibson), carried him to the hospital. Bob wondered whether he would die, and Josh told him, "No, Robert, you're not going to die. And when you're well, I'm going to buy you a bat and glove." Of course, he did recover, and he became a late-blooming star in basketball as well as baseball. In fact, he was on a college all-star team that played the Harlem Globetrotters, a team that hardly ever loses. Bob sat on the bench for three quarters while the Globetrotters took and held the lead, and then in the fourth quarter he came into the game and scored 15 points to lead his team to a one-point victory. The impressed Globetrotters immediately offered him a contract to play for them, and he did for four months, in 1957-1958, earning $4,000.[129]

• Early in her skating career, Sasha Cohen collided with another skater on a practice rink. Her leg didn't feel right, so she went off the ice to examine the wound. Blood was present, and Sasha felt squeamish, but fortunately an older figure skater, Jenni Meno, came by and knew exactly what to do and say to reassure her: "It's OK, you're fine, it's gonna be fine." Unfortunately a younger figure skater, Naomi Nari Nam, came by, and she didn't know what to say to reassure her: "OH, MY GOD! WHAT HAPPENED? THERE'S A HUGE HOLE IN YOUR LEG!" Sasha ended up at the hospital and got 21 stitches.[130]

• An accident can end the career of an athlete very quickly. Maureen Connolly, a USAmerican tennis player, won singles championships at Wimbledon in 1952, 1953, and 1954. In addition, she became the first woman ever to win the Grand Slam, by winning the major championships in four different countries — Australia, England, France, and the United States — in 1953. But while she was riding a horse at home during a break from tennis, a truck sideswiped her horse and severely injured her right leg. Suddenly, her tennis career was over.[131]

• In 1991, Pittsburgh Penguin hockey player Mario Lemieux scored a goal and made three assists as Pittsburgh defeated the Minnesota North Stars and won the Stanley Cup. As recognition for his efforts throughout the playoffs, Mr. Lemieux was voted Most Valuable Player. However, before the game, he suffered from so much back pain that he was unable to tie his own skate laces.[132]

• As heavyweight champion Rocky Marciano played with his baby daughter, Mary Ann, throwing her into the air and catching her, he wrenched his back. His physician examined him and told him that if he continued to fight, he might never walk properly again, so Mr. Marciano retired undefeated.[133]

• A surgeon once removed a huge bone chip from the ankle of USAmerican gymnast Vanessa Atler, and he was shocked by its size, even after having worked for years on the injuries of the Dallas Cowboys. Ms. Atler joked, "See, that makes me tougher than all those football players."[134]

• A Toronto infielder named Al Brancato once arrived at the ballpark with a bad limp. His manager asked what had happened, and Mr. Brancato said, "I bruised my knee." The manager asked how, and Mr. Brancato explained, "Kneeling in church this morning."[135]

• On a TV quiz show, Joe Garagiola asked Hugh Downs about his first impression of his wife. Mr. Downs replied, "Immoral," then explained, "I was hit on the knee by a golf ball and she said it was a good thing it wasn't any higher. She meant harder."[136]

Language

• Some controversies involve words. At a Mississippi high school, parents of the players on the football team were upset because they said the coach had called the players "chicken****," so they held a meeting in an attempt to get the coach fired. Country comedian Jerry Clower's wife, Homerline, stood up at the meeting and said, "I was trying to think of what word would describe the way they played the other night, and that's the word."[137]

• Chinese gymnast Li Ning decided to learn English as part of his preparation for the 1984 Olympic Games in Los Angeles. When he told his friends on the U.S. gymnastics team — through a translator

— they laughed, because English is notoriously hard to learn unless you grow up speaking it. However, months later U.S. gymnast Mitch Gaylord sneezed, and Li Ning astonished the U.S. gymnasts by saying, "God bless you."[138]

Mascots

• Animal mascots can play a big role in college football. Handsome Dan XIII, a bulldog, was the mascot of Yale University. When his keeper, Chris Getman, would ask him which he preferred, going to Harvard University or being dead, Handsome Dan XIII would roll on his back and pretend to be dead. One of Handsome Dan's predecessors was Handsome Dan II, who was dognapped the day before the Harvard-Yale football game in 1934. The dastardly Harvards photographed Handsome Dan II licking the boots of a statue of the man whom Harvard is named after: John Harvard. (The boots had been smeared with hamburger.) Yale won, 14-0, but the Yalies still felt humiliated by their mascot, and the Yale crew team even adopted another bulldog as its mascot, resulting in what is known as the canine Great Schism.[139]

• The mascot of the University of Georgia Bulldogs is — you guessed it — a bulldog. The bulldogs' name — several bulldogs have served as mascots — is Uga, which derives from the abbreviation of the University of Georgia: U of GA. Unfortunately, one problem did arise for the mascots. Georgia weather is hot, even during the football season, and it is especially hot for English Bulldogs. Fortunately, the Bahamian Bulldog Club of Nassau, which is located in the Bahama Islands, solved the problem by providing Uga with his very own air-conditioned doghouse in the football arena.[140]

Media

• Bill Nack was sports editor and then editor of *The Daily Illini*, the school newspaper of the University of Illinois at Urbana-Champaign. He loved horses and while he was sports editor and Roger Ebert was editor, he ran stories on all of the major horse races. Mr. Ebert remembers, "We had only one photo of a horse. We used it for every winner. If it was a filly, we flipped it. Of this as his editor I approved." Mr. Nack served in Vietnam and then started writing for *Newsday*. At a *Newsday* holiday party, he stood on a desk and recited from memory the winners of the Kentucky Derby — every race, complete with names and dates. Dave Laventhiol, *Newsday* editor, asked him why he knew that information. Mr. Nack replied, "It's the Damon Runyan in me." Mr. Laventhiol then offered Mr. Nack his dream job: "Would you like to cover the races for *Newsday*?" In five minutes, he had the job, but he did have to write a note asking for the job so that Mr. Laventhiol could post it on the bulletin board for the curious who would wonder why Mr. Nack was making a radical change in what he wrote about for *Newsday*. In the note, Mr. Nack wrote, "After covering politicians for four years, I would like the chance to cover the whole horse."[141]

• In 1987, the Los Angeles Lakers won the first two games of the NBA Championships, beating the Boston Celtics. Lakers great Magic Johnson worried after the second game that his teammates, including Michael Cooper, were spending too much time talking to reporters — something that can lead to cockiness and overconfidence, which are not what you want to have when facing a tough opponent. Magic whispered to Michael to end the interview. Michael kept talking, so Magic tapped Michael on the shoulder and told him it was time to end the interview — *now*. This could have led to a disagreement between teammates, but Michael respected Magic, so he smiled and ended the interview, telling the reporters, "Well, you heard him." The Lakers won the 1987 NBA Championship four games to two.[142]

• At one time, sportswriters were a wild and crazy bunch who used to have fun. For example, Texas sportswriters Gary Cartwright, Blackie Sherrod, and Bud Shrake used to wear capes and leotards and pretend to be Les Flying Punzars, acrobatic Italians who came from a mysterious somewhere. Their speciality was the triple somersault, which unfortunately they were always unable to perform because they lacked a trapeze. By the way, Mr. Sherrod used to refer to sports as the "perspiring arts."[143]

• Hugh Troy once worked as a sports reporter for the student newspaper at Cornell. As a reporter, he gave the newspaper the reports of track and field meets, but he felt bad for whoever finished last in an event. Therefore, he invented the name "Johnny Tsal" and always listed Johnny Tsal as finishing last in whatever event he was covering.[144]

• After ice skater Katerina Witt performed a sultry routine to *Carmen* at the 1988 Olympic Games in Calgary, she attended a press conference, where a USAmerican reporter started the questioning by asking, "Will you marry me?"[145]

Chapter 4: From Mishaps to Pitchers

Mishaps

• Casey Stengel once had a rookie who was very fast, but who couldn't play well. Still, he was so fast that Casey kept the rookie on the roster to use as a pinch runner. The rookie didn't play much, but a game came up in which Casey needed a speedy base runner on second, and in the rookie went. Casey was relieved when a player hit a long ball, for the speedy rookie could easily run home and score the winning run. However, the rookie slipped while rounding third and didn't make it home, instead staying on third. The inning ended with the rookie still on third. When Casey asked the rookie what had happened, the rookie almost cried as he explained, "I figured I wouldn't get to play anyway, so I wore shoes without spikes so I'd be comfortable."[146]

• The Boy Scouts' motto is "Be Prepared." In 1954, Giants' back-up quarterback Bobby Clatterbuck was not prepared when Charley Conerly tore some ligaments in his knee during a game and Mr. Clatterbuck had to go in the game to replace him. Mr. Clatterbuck's vision was not perfect, and he wore eyeglasses off the football field and contact lens on the football field. For this game, he had been sure that he would ride the bench all game the way he usually did, and he was not wearing his contact lens, which were in the dressing room. The Giants lost to the Cleveland Browns, 16-7.[147]

• Lynette Woodard's cousin Hubert "Geese" Ausbie played for the Harlem Globetrotters, and when she was young, he taught her many of the tricks the Globetrotters played with a basketball, including a trick where she let the basketball roll from one arm to another across her shoulders. This trick had a deleterious effect on Lynette's house while she was growing up. She says, "I kind of tore up the house doing it. Well, not the whole house, but the lamp, the iron, the ashtray, the window in my room."[148]

• In an NFL football game, Walter Payton went up the middle, was tackled, and lay on the ground and wouldn't get up. A teammate asked, "Are you hurt?" Mr. Payton replied, "No, but I'm not getting up. Go and get the equipment manager." The equipment manager came out, spoke to Mr. Payton, then returned to the bench and got a big towel. Soon, the mystery was explained. Mr. Payton had split his pants and was too embarrassed to get up without a towel to cover his rear end.[149]

• While serving in the Romanian army as required by law, world-class women's gymnastics coach Bela Karolyi was given the task of hauling around a huge, heavy machine gun mounted on wheels. This was tiring work and after hauling the machine up a hill, Mr. Karolyi decided to ride the machine gun down the hill. He climbed up on it, rode it down, and nearly ran over his commanding officer.[150]

• Lord Snowden was a photographer. In 1957, he posed the Queen of England and her royal consort in an outdoor sporting situation. To serve as part of the scene in the photograph, he had purchased a few dead trout, but they didn't appear in the photograph. On the day of the photo shoot, Lord Snowden's housekeeper found the trout, cooked them, and served them to him for breakfast.[151]

• Rube Waddell was a farm boy who made it as a big-league pitcher, but he had some learning to do in his early days in professional baseball. In an early game, the batter hit the ball back to him, but instead of throwing the ball to the first baseman, he threw it at the runner — hard. The opposing team protested, of course, but Rube simply said, "Where I come from, that's an out."[152]

• Clyde "Bulldog" Turner used to play center for the Chicago Bears. At a party, he fell out of a 3rd-floor window and would have been killed if not for an awning, which broke his fall. A police officer saw him fall, and ran over to him, demanding, "What's going on?" Bulldog picked himself up and said, "I don't know, officer. I just got here myself."[153]

• At a party, a little-old-lady friend of Canadian figure skater Toller Cranston tried — and liked — mescaline. Afterward, she went to her pharmacy and ordered mescaline, only to be told by the pharmacist, "Madame, I am sorry, but that drug is highly illegal." She replied, "But when I snorted it last night, it did wonders for my sinuses."[154]

• When teenager Evelyn Cornwall (later, she changed her name to Lyn St. James) tore down and rebuilt her first car, she had a bucket of parts left over. This made her feel bad — until another mechanic told her, "It happens all the time." Later, she became only the second woman to drive a car in the Indianapolis 500.[155]

• Beach volleyballers often dive in the sand to prevent a point by the other team. The best volleyballers, such as Misty May-Treanor and Kerri Walsh, sometimes have sand on their lips but not in their mouths. Ms. May-Treanor explains, "You have to dive with your mouth closed. If you do, it saves on the dental work."[156]

• Boxer Sonny Tufts once complained about the newspaper media on a live radio program. He said, "I don't give a godd*mn what newspaper people write about me. ... I'm awfully sorry about my language. ... Really, I'm godd*mned sorry."[157]

Money

• Chicago baseball player Ernie Banks grew up in Dallas as one of 11 children. Money was scarce, and grocery shopping often resulted in carrying lots of beans and rice home. When Mr. Banks got $2,000 to sign with the Cubs, he telephoned his father to say, "We're rich." Mr. Banks played before baseball stars got mega-million-dollar contracts, but his boss, William Wrigley, Jr., of chewing gum fame, offered to set up a trust fund for each of his players. Mr. Banks took him up on his offer. Half of Mr. Banks' salary went into his trust fund, and he couldn't touch his trust-fund money until he was 55 years old. At that time, he had $4 million — good money then as now. Mr. Wrigley also helped Mr. Banks become the first African American to own a Ford dealership. Mr. Banks managed his money well. He once ended an interview with sportswriter Steve Jacobson after receiving a telephone call — Mr. Banks had to leave to see about buying a bank.[158]

• When pitcher Greg Maddux was signed by the Chicago Cubs out of high school, he received a signing bonus of $82,000. Because of this, Mr. Maddux decided not to go to college; however, he was very careful with the money. He knew that if he did not make it in the major leagues, he could use the money to go to college, so he put it in the bank and lived on his small salary as a minor-league player, promising himself that he would not touch the $82,000 until he either left baseball after failing to make it or until he had made it into the major leagues. He did exactly what he had promised himself he would do; fortunately, he did not have to wait too long until he made it into the major leagues.[159]

• Yousouf, aka the Terrible Turk, made his living as a wrestler. He always requested that he be paid in gold, which he kept in a belt that he wore around his waist. On 15 January 1910, in Canada Yousouf wrestled a man named Chaaker. The wrestling match ended with a victory for Yousouf, but unfortunately, minutes after Chaaker was pinned, he died. Yousouf immediately retired from wrestling, and he boarded a ship that was sailing back home to his native Turkey. On its second day at sea, the ship ran into a storm and started to sink. Yousouf jumped into the sea near a lifeboat, but the weight of the gold in his belt pulled him into the sea and he drowned.[160]

• Dodger executive Branch Rickey was a tight man when it came to giving salaries to his ballplayers. If a player had a great year, Mr. Rickey would tell him, "Well, son, you had a nice year. We decided to let you come back." When Tommy Lasorda was in the Dodgers' minor leagues, he negotiated a contract with Mr. Rickey and came up on the losing side. When Mr. Rickey suggested that the terms of the contract remain "just between us," Mr. Lasorda replied, "You don't need to worry about me saying anything to anyone about my salary. I'm just as ashamed of it as you are."[161]

• When he was playing in the minor leagues, baseball star Bobby Bonilla decided to get married. He asked his girlfriend, Millie Quiñones, to come to where he was playing so they could get married. She did, and he gave her $22 — almost all the money he had — so she could buy a dress and shoes to be married in. Of course, $22 doesn't go very far, and the shoes she bought were so cheap that they turned her feet grey. Three years later, in 1988, Mr. Bonilla was playing in the major leagues for the Pittsburg Pirates and making a $230,000 annual salary.[162]

• The decathlon is a grueling event, and after Bob Mathias won a gold medal in the decathlon at the 1948 Olympic Games, his first words were these: "I wouldn't do this again for a million dollars." However, the pain of winning an Olympic gold medal in the decathlon must be a lot like the pain of giving birth. The reward is so great that often the pain is willingly endured again. Many mothers have a second child, and four years later Mr. Mathias competed in the 1952 Olympic games and won a second gold medal in the decathlon.[163]

• Families sometimes have to sacrifice to enable their children to become national- and world-class athletes. Before figure skater Kristi Yamaguchi competed at the 1992 United States National Championships, her mother said, "There have been financial sacrifices to get where we are. We all drive old cars with over 160,000 miles." Nevertheless, Kristi's mother had enough money to offer her $100 if she made a difficult triple salchow. Going into the jump, Kristi told herself, "Just do it and get the hundred bucks." She did.[164]

• While attending Florida State University, Gabrielle Reece worked as a model at the same time she played on the volleyball team. In fact, she gave up her athletic scholarship because athletes weren't allowed both to work and to have a scholarship. However, she never let work interfere with her duties as an athlete during the volleyball season. She points out, "I would never go on a job during the season. I turned down one job — $35,000 for two days' work — because I had a game."[165]

• In 1955, Roberto Clemente's team, the Pittsburgh Pirates, were not winning games; therefore, Mr. Clemente took out his frustrations on the team's plastic batting helmets, smashing 22 of them. Manager Fred Haney threatened to start charging him $10 for each batting helmet he destroyed, and Mr. Clemente, whose first language was Spanish, decided to start controlling his temper, saying, "I do not make so much money. I'll stop breaking the hats."[166]

• Garry Payton of the NBA Seattle SuperSonics was once dared to shoot a basket during a game by a defender. Mr. Payton shot, made a 3-pointer, then told the defender, "That's why I make $12 million."[167]

Mothers

• Bill Russell's mother was tough, and she expected her son to be tough, too. When Bill was nine years old, he and his mother moved to Oakland, California, to join his father, who had gotten a job there. While Bill was outside in the Housing Authority project where he lived, five kids ran by him, and one of the kids slapped him. He told his mother what had happened, and she went with him to find all five kids. When Bill said that they had found the five kids, she said, "Good, because you are going to fight all of them, one at a time." Bill won two fights, and he lost the other three, but his mother told him, "Don't you feel bad now, William. You did right. You stood up for yourself like a man. Always stand up for yourself like a man." As a member of the Boston Celtics, Bill played 13 seasons, and he and the Celtics won 11 championships.[168]

• Olympic gold medal-winning figure skater Tara Lipinski is named after the plantation in *Gone With the Wind*. Her parents had seen the movie on an early date, and her mother named her Tara because of the good things that came from that early date.[169]

Names

• Jim Thorpe's mausoleum is located in Jim Thorpe, Pennsylvania. The town used to be known as the separate small towns of Mauch Chunk and East Mauch Chunk, but after hard economic times hit the towns because coal mining declined, the residents started looking for ways to draw industry and attention to their area. Mr. Thorpe's widow heard about their situation and offered to move the body of her husband there if they would rename the two towns after Jim Thorpe. They did so, and they provided money for a mausoleum for Mr. Thorpe. At the May 31, 1957, dedication ceremony, earth from parts of the world that had been important in Mr. Thorpe's life was scattered around the mausoleum. Earth was scattered from his birthplace in Prague, Oklahoma; from the Polo Grounds, where he had played professional baseball with the New York Giants; and from the Olympic Stadium in Stockholm, Sweden, where Mr. Thorpe had won gold medals in the pentathlon and decathlon.[170]

• In pro-wrestling jargon, the wrestlers that fans cheer are babyfaces, while the wrestlers that fans jeer are heels. Sometimes, one wrestler can be both a babyface and a heel. Bret "Hit Man" Hart is from Canada, and at one time his wrestling persona heavily criticized the United States, saying such things as this: "Canada's a country where we still take care of the sick and the old, where we still have health care. We got gun control. We don't kill each other and shoot each other on every street corner. Canada isn't riddled with racial prejudice and hatred." In Canada, people were very happy with what he was saying, so there he was a babyface. In the United States, people were very unhappy with what he was saying, so there he was a heel.[171]

• Minor-league umpire Jack Gifford once finished talking with the team managers about ground rules, then bent down and started to brush what he thought was the home plate, but no matter how much he brushed, the home plate did not appear. A ball player watched him for a while, and then said, "The plate is over here." Mr. Gifford then looked up and saw home plate, several feet away. After that, of course, the baseball players called him "Home Plate" Gifford.[172]

• Evelyn Cornwall married John Carusso, then divorced him. Thinking she needed a name change, she considered a favorite television show, *McMillan and Wife*, starring Susan St. James. She telephoned the famous actress, asked for permission to use her last name, then legally changed her name and became Lyn St. James. The name change may have been lucky for her — she became only the second woman to drive a car in the Indianapolis 500.[173]

• When Joe Louis was heavyweight champion of the world before World War II broke out, he often fought, and he often won by knocking out his opponents. Longtime fighter trainer Ray Arcel handled 14 fighters who opposed Mr. Louis during this time. Mr. Arcel carried so many of these knocked-out fighters out of the ring that he acquired a nickname: The Meat Wagon.[174]

• When she was growing up, Karen Bye wanted to play on a boys' hockey team in River Falls, Wisconsin. To facilitate her plan, she listed her name as "K.L. Bye" on the team roster. Today, she is still sometimes called "K.L." At the 1998 Nagano Olympic Games, K.L. became a gold-medal winner as a member of the United States women's hockey team.[175]

• At the 1964 Olympic Games in Tokyo, Japan, Native American Billy Mills pulled off a major upset when he won the 10,000-meter race. His victory was so unexpected that after Mr. Mills won the race, a Japanese race official was forced to ask him, "Excuse me, what is your name?"[176]

Numbers

• NBA star Kobe Bryant played basketball for Lower Merion High School (located in Ardmore, Pennsylvania), which became state champions in his senior year. During his junior year, Lower Merion High School had a good basketball season, but the team lost to Chester High School, 77-50. In the rematch between the two schools, the

Lower Merion High School players all wore the number "27" on their warm-up jerseys — the number of points they had lost by in their previous game with Chester High School. This time, Lower Merion High School won, 60-53, and kept on winning until they earned a state championship. Later, Kobe became a Los Angeles Laker right out of high school. On 11 July 1996, at Los Angeles Airport, a man looked at Kobe's height and knew that he must be a basketball player, so he asked for which team he played. Kobe almost replied that he played for Lower Merion High School, but then he smiled and said, "I guess I'm a Laker."[177]

• While playing for the Laval Voisins of the Quebec Major Junior Hockey League, Pittsburgh Penguin hockey player Mario Lemieux wanted to honor his hero, professional hockey player Wayne Gretzky, by wearing his number, 99. However, Mr. Lemieux' agent, Bob Perno, suggested that instead he turn Mr. Gretzky's number upside down and wear number 66. That's exactly what Mr. Lemieux did while playing for both the Laval Voisins and the Pittsburgh Penguins.[178]

Olympics

• Marla Runyan is legally blind in both eyes, but that did not keep her from being an athlete. At age nine, she started having trouble seeing. Eventually, a doctor diagnosed her with a rare disease that attacks the retina: Stargardt's Disease. Fortunately, she was able to go to school even with diminished eyesight. Her parents bought her an instrument called a monocular so that she could see the blackboard, and they bought her a machine that displayed the words of books very large on a television screen so that she could read them. Grady, her brother, also helped. When it was time to her to go to high school, he took her all around the school. That way, she was able to memorize the positions of her classrooms. She did have one problem, though. She was very good at getting around by herself, and sometimes people thought that she was snobbish because she did not greet them. They didn't realize that she couldn't see them well enough to recognize them.

A track star, she competed for the United States in the 1,500-meter race at the 2000 Olympic Games in Sydney, Australia. She was the first legally blind Olympian.[179]

• Of course, the Atlanta Olympic Organizing Committee wanted someone special to light the Olympic flame at the 1996 Olympic Games in Atlanta, Georgia, and they decided to ask Muhammad Ali to do it. However, they wanted it to be a secret, so they decided to meet secretly with Mr. Ali's friend Howard Bingham, with emphasis on the word "secretly" — if anyone were to see them meeting Mr. Bingham, the secret would be out. Therefore, Billy Paine, the head of the Atlanta Olympic Organizing Committee, and Don Mischer, producer of the opening ceremonies, met with Mr. Bingham in a garbage room — the garbage had been pushed out of the way to make room for some chairs and a table. Mr. Bingham agreed to ask Mr. Ali if he would light the flame, and Mr. Ali was honored by the request.[180]

• Australian Murray Rose and Japanese Tsuyoshi Yamanaka were teammates together at USC, but they swam against each other at the 1956 Olympic Games in Melbourne, Australia. Although a Japanese team was competing in Australia, World War II had been over for only 11 years, and many people remembered when Australians were worried about being invaded by the Japanese during the war. Mr. Rose and Mr. Yamanaka competed in the 1,500-meter freestyle, and despite a strong finish by Mr. Yamanaka, Mr. Rose won by two meters. The two men then embraced each other in the water, resulting in a photograph that was widely reproduced in Australia and elsewhere. One of the captions in Australia said, "The war is finally over."[181]

• If you had a chance to compete in the Olympics, would you turn it down? Tara Dakides did. Her sport is snowboarding, and she declined to compete in the 1998 Winter Olympic Games in Japan because she didn't like the rules of the competition. Snowboarders were supposed to make two runs, not three, leading to athletes playing it safe. Ms. Dakides believes that snowboarding is all about taking risks, so she stayed away from the Olympics. By the way, Louise A. Gikow, the woman who wrote about Ms. Dakides in the children's book *Extreme Sports*, owns cats that engage in extreme sports — they jump down from high furniture without wearing parachutes.[182]

• Tim Daggett's first encounter with gymnastics was by pure accident. He played a different sport, and as he was walking down a school hallway one day he looked into the gym and saw someone doing giant swings on the high bars. The gymnast let go of the bar, flew high in the air, performed a back flip, and then landed gracefully on his feet. Tim was impressed enough to devote much of the next 17 years of his life to gymnastics, and at the 1984 Olympics, he scored a perfect 10 on high bar to clinch team gold for the United States men's gymnastics team.[183]

• When Muhammad Ali was still known as Cassius Clay, he almost did not make it to the 1960 Olympic Games in Rome to win a gold medal as a light heavyweight. Why not? He was afraid of flying. Eventually, Joe Martin, his trainer, convinced him that he had to fly, so Cassius boarded the airplane — carrying his own parachute, which he had bought at an Army surplus store. Even with the parachute, he was still nervous. At one point, he knelt down in the aisle of the airplane while wearing the parachute and prayed.[184]

• In 1998, at the Olympic Games in Nagano, Japan, Tara Lipinski won the gold medal. Her parents wanted her to enjoy all that the Olympics had to offer, so Tara stayed in the Olympic Village with the other athletes. She enjoyed marching in the opening ceremony and met such famous athletes as hockey's Wayne Gretzky. In addition, the 79-pound Tara posed for a photograph with a sumo wrestler who weighed 516 pounds — six and a half times her weight![185]

• At the opening ceremonies of the 1992 Winter Olympic Games, figure skater Sasha Cohen was lucky enough to sit next to President George W. Bush. She called her mother to tell her, but her mother didn't believe her, so Sasha handed her cell phone to President Bush, who spoke to Sasha's mother for a few minutes. (President Bush may not have enjoyed watching the Opening Ceremonies — lots of athletes kept passing their cell phones to him and requesting that he talk to someone.)[186]

• Before the 1984 Olympics, gymnast Mary Lou Retton used to dream that she was performing in the Olympics. She would be lying in bed asleep, then suddenly her body would jerk, and she would be at risk of falling out of bed onto the floor.[187]

• The Big Apple Circus once did a parody of the Olympics. The clowns put ice down their pants, and then exhibited their skill in ice dancing.[188]

Pitchers

• In 1954, Dodger pitcher Carl Erskine faced Mickey Vernon. With the count at three balls and one strike, catcher Smokey Burgess called for an unusual pitch in that situation: a straight change. The pitch was perfect, and Mr. Vernon had strike two. Apparently, the straight change was such a surprise to Mr. Vernon that he let a fastball go across the plate for his final strike. Mr. Erskine and Mr. Vernon did not see each other for 25 years after that, finally meeting again at an Old-Timers' Game weekend. When Mr. Vernon saw Mr. Erskine, he walked over to him and said, "That was a helluva pitch."[189]

• The St. Louis Cardinals, aka the Gas House Gang, once faced a poor-pitching team whose starting pitcher walked four Cardinals in a row before being yanked. The next pitcher also fared poorly, walking two Cardinals and hitting two more Cardinals with balls. Batting ninth for the Cardinals was pitcher Dizzy Dean, who hit a weak grounder back to the pitcher, who misfielded the ball, allowing Dizzy to reach first safely. At first base, Dizzy complained, "A fine team I'm playing on. It isn't enough that I do the pitching, I have to do the hitting, too."[190]

• As a major-league pitcher, Virgil "Fire" Trucks threw two no-hitters, but his career started inauspiciously. In 1942, in his first start as a major-leaguer, Mr. Trucks threw his first pitch against Johnny Pesky, who singled. He threw his second pitch against Bobby Doer, who doubled, and he threw his third pitch against Ted Williams, who also doubled. At this point, the Detroit Tigers manager came out to ask the catcher, "Doesn't Virgil have it today?" "How do I know?" the catcher replied, "I haven't caught a pitch yet."[191]

• Truett "Rip" Sewell well remembers the first game he pitched against the great slugger Stan Musial. The first three times Mr. Musial was batting, he got a hit, including the first home run of his major-league career. The fourth time Mr. Musial came up to bat in the game, Mr. Sewell rolled the ball to home plate, and yelled to Mr. Musial, "Here! Hit this one!" The following year, Mr. Musial hit his first grand-slam home run — of course, he hit it against Mr. Sewell.[192]

• Ohio farmboy Denton Tecumseh Young had a fastball so speedy that he became known as "Cyclone" Young, which later was shortened to Cy Young. He was quite a pitcher, winning 30 or more games five seasons in a row, and winning 20 or more games 14 seasons in a row. When he retired, he had won 511 games. He could still pitch extremely well, but he decided to quit because he could not field bunts — he had grown too fat![193]

• Bob Feller threw hard, and definitely hard enough to hurt. Early in his career he was preparing to face Lefty Gomez in the late innings of a game as the evening was growing dark. Stepping up the plate, Lefty lit a match. Umpire Bill Sommers asked, "What's the matter, Gomez? Can't you see Feller?" Lefty replied, "I can see him all right — I just want to make sure that he can see me."[194]

• Dizzy Dean was a talented pitcher for the St. Louis Cardinals. In the 1934 World Series, in the ninth inning of the final game of the series, the Detroit team sent the great hitter Hank Greenberg to bat against him, but Dizzy said loudly, "What's the matter? Ain't you people got no peench hitters?" Then Dizzy struck him out.[195]

• The great African-American pitcher Satchel Paige sometimes would call in his outfielders and have them sit down behind the pitchers mound. He then would strike out the batters facing him. Some people considered this a kind of bragging, but Satchel always replied, "If you can do it, it ain't bragging."[196]

• Robin Roberts once struck out three Pittsburgh Pirates in a row after a player hit a triple. He struck out Pete Castiglione with five pitches, Ralph Kiner with four pitches, and Joe Garagiola with three pitches. Afterward, Mr. Garagiola said, "It's embarrassing. He should have at least *worked* on me."[197]

Chapter 5: From Practical Jokes to World

Practical Jokes

• Practical jokes are a part of life of minor-league baseball, with rookies often the target — and often the rookies try to get their own back. Matt Smith was the new pitcher for the Birmingham Barons, and veteran Jake Meyer dumped a bucket of ice water on him when Matt was in the shower. Jaker then said, "Welcome to the bullpen." Another veteran, Brian West, advised Matt to throw ice water on Jake the next day at 5 p.m. when Jake would be in the shower. Matt promised to do that, and he did just that, throwing the ice water on Jake and then running out of the shower. Unfortunately, he heard a loud crash, and suddenly baseball players started screaming for the trainer. Jake came out of the shower with two players assisting him. Lots of blood was flowing down from his head, and the manager, Wally Backman, looked at him and said, "We have to get him to the hospital. We have to get him stitched up." Then Wally asked who was responsible. Everybody pointed at Matt, who said, "Wally, I didn't mean to do anything." Wally chewed Matt out, and Matt was afraid that he is going to be fired. Then he noticed that Jake was furious and trying to get at him, but he couldn't because two players were holding him back. Wally, noticing the same thing, said, "Let him go. He's got to do what he's got to do." Jake came at Matt, but instead of hitting him, he put a tube of fake blood in his hand. Brian had told the entire team that Matt was going to throw ice water on Jake, and the entire team was in on the practical joke on a very relieved Matt, who admitted, "It was the most elaborate, choreographed prank I've heard of."[198]

• Fielding Yost, a football coach at the University of Michigan, took sides in the then-current controversy of who had discovered the North Pole: Doc Cook or Commodore Perry. Mr. Yost believed that Commodore Perry had discovered the North Pole, and he was ready at any time to argue the case for Perry. Knowing this, Dan McGugin, the brother-in-law of Mr. Yost and a football coach at Vanderbilt, set up a practical joke. Mr. Yost, Mr. McGugin, and a group of their friends started talking about the Cook-Perry controversy, and they took a vote to see which side everyone took in the controversy. The vote was 18 to 3 that Commodore Perry was the true discover of the North Pole. Therefore, Mr. Yost argued well and passionately in an attempt to convince the three non-believers that Commodore Perry was the true discover of the North Pole. At the end of Mr. Yost's 40-minute speech, another vote was held. This time, with the sole exception of Mr. Yost, the vote was in favor of Doc Cook. On another occasion, Mr. Yost was scheduled to give a speech to the National Coaches Association. He believed in being prepared, so he worked hard writing and memorizing his speech, and he even practiced his speech a few times in front of Mr. McGugin, who was also attending the meeting. However, just before Mr. Yost spoke at the meeting, Mr. McGugin stood up and gave Mr. Yost's speech, leaving him to improvise a new speech as best he could.[199]

• In 1987, catcher Dave Bresnahan became famous briefly for throwing a potato in Class AA baseball in Williamsport, Pennsylvania. He had peeled a potato so that it was round like a baseball, then hid it in an extra baseball glove in the dugout. When an opposing player reached third base, Mr. Bresnahan told the umpire that his glove was broken, and went to the dugout to get his potato and spare glove. He then pretended to try to throw the player out at third base with a wild throw, that player ran home to score a run, and Mr. Bresnahan tagged him with the real baseball. The umpire was plenty mad when he found out what had happened, and he let the runner score although Mr. Bresnahan argued, "You can't give him a run on a wildly thrown potato. Can you? Look it up." Unfortunately for Mr. Bresnahan, he was fired for his stunt, although the farm director laughed and said, "That was ingenious. What are you trying to do: get on the David Letterman show?"[200]

• On 6 July 1936, 17-year-old Bob Feller got to pitch in an exhibition game for the Cleveland Indians as they played the St. Louis Cardinals. Bob used his blazing fastball as he struck out Leo Durocher in three pitches. Yes, Bob's fastball was blazing, but another thing that helped him was an occasional lack of control that allowed the ball to go toward the batter instead of the catcher, as previous batters had learned. After striking out, Leo went to the dugout and hid behind the water cooler while yelling at Bob, "You can't hit me from here!" Bob was capable of joking around as well. Later, he used to attach noisy — but harmless — bombs to the cars of guests attending parties at his home. Some bombs made a bang when the owners started their cars, and some bombs that were attached to the tires made bangs as the cars traveled down the road.[201]

• Professional baseball player Truett "Rip" Sewell once roomed with a practical joker and outfielder named "Junk" Walters. Junk once snuck up on Rip in the shower and smeared his rear end with a salve that was used to heat injuries. Rip would sit down, then stand up, then sit down — because of the salve, he couldn't get comfortable. Later, when they were playing in Oakland, California, Rip was lying in bed when it began to move. He was sure that Junk was up to some devilment or other, so he said, "Junk, cut that out!" Junk replied, "You better shut up, Sewell, and stand in this doorway with me — we're having an earthquake!"[202]

• At the beginning of the NCAA gymnastics meet in 1974, a man walked out onto the floor exercise mat wearing nothing but pantyhose — over his head. Otherwise completely nude, he performed a roundoff, a back handspring, and a back somersault, and then he raced away with a police officer in pursuit. After managing to elude the police officer, he removed the pantyhose mask, got dressed, and returned to watch the competition. The nude gymnast was Jim Culhane, who made $35 in dares for performing his stunt.[203]

• Nolan Ryan was one out away from a no-hitter when practical joker Norm Cash came up to bat, but he didn't have a bat — he had a table leg! Even though Mr. Cash claimed that the way that Mr. Nolan was pitching, a bat wouldn't do him any good, umpire Ron Luciano made him step up the plate with a real bat. Actually, Mr. Cash was right — the bat didn't help him. Mr. Cash popped up, and Mr. Nolan recorded a no-hitter.[204]

• Hockey is a rough sport, and many hockey players wear dentures. On an away trip, mid-1970s player Bob Plager of the St. Louis Blues once stole the dentures of his teammate Larry Keenan and mailed them to Mr. Keenan's home. During a different game, after Mr. Plager was sent to the locker room because of game misconduct, he visited his teammates' lockers and switched around their dentures.[205]

Prejudice

• Gene Sarazen was born Eugene Saraceni. When he was playing professional golf in the 1920s, some of the other golfers did not want to play with an Italian. For example, at the 1922 U.S. Open, a golfer named Jim Barnes made a fuss about playing a practice round with him. However, Mr. Sarazen won the U.S. Open, and he and Jim Barnes were scheduled to play an exhibition match together for money. Jim Barnes asked Mr. Sarazen if he wanted to split the purse evenly no matter who won, but Mr. Sarazen declined. To make a point, he wanted to beat Jim Barnes in the exhibition match and take all the money — which he did.[206]

• When Muhammad Ali, then known as Cassius Clay, won a gold medal at the Olympic Games in Rome in 1960, he wore it all the time, even sleeping with it. (He started sleeping on his back so that the medal wouldn't cut his chest.) However, even with Olympic gold, he still faced prejudice. In Louisville, Kentucky, he and an African-American friend went to a restaurant. There, they were refused service because of their race, even though Mr. Clay showed the owner of the restaurant his gold medal.[207]

• Barbara Jo Rubin hit the big time as a woman jockey — the first one to do so. However, she had to overcome prejudice before fully making her mark. Early in her career, 11 male jockeys boycotted a race she was supposed to ride in, forcing its cancellation. Fortunately, each male jockey was fined $100, with the promise of stiffer fines to come if they continued to boycott races in which a woman jockey was scheduled to compete.[208]

• Pittsburgh Pirate (and Baseball Hall of Famer) Roberto Clemente sometimes felt that he was being discriminated against in southern cities. When that happened, he would tell the clerk his identity, watch as the prejudice turned into awe and compliments, and then leave.[209]

Problem-Solving

• When Paul "Bear" Bryant coached for the University of Kentucky, a fumble occurred in a game against the University of Tennessee. Unfortunately, the fumble occurred near the Kentucky bench, where a box of footballs was knocked over. The footballs rolled onto the playing field, and the football players recovered them. Because the referees had no way of telling which football was the real game ball, they awarded possession to the University of Tennessee — whose players had recovered five of the nine footballs on the field. By the way, the author of this book originally wrote "Paul "Bryant" Bryant. Marty Pflugrath of Bartcop Entertainment emailed me and wrote, "I think that should be Paul "Bear" Bryant. His name is well known where I grew up — my little town's largest industry is a paper mill, owned, at that time, by Curtis Publishing. When Bryant sued the *Saturday Evening Post* (owned by Curtis Publishing) and won, the mill was shut down for a while, then sold several times, each time requiring fewer employees. Sixty-some years later I still know people who spit after they say his name." Marty added in a later email, "Pretty much everything revolved around the mill, and that sale changed everything — people moved away, businesses, like the movie theater, bowling alley, and shoe store closed. It's an area where liquor licenses are coveted, and even bars closed. A firsthand look at what one man can do. Sigh."[210]

• During the Jim Crow days, professional baseball player Ed Charles, an African American, and his white teammates (and one black teammate) stopped in rural Georgia. The black ballplayers were not allowed to eat in the restaurant, so their white teammates brought out food for them to eat on the team bus. But of course the white teammates could not go to the restroom for them. Mr. Charles was angry, so he entered the "Whites Only" restroom and a white employee entered and started hassling him. One of Mr. Charles' white teammates entered the restroom and got in the white employee's face, then a second white teammate entered the restroom and got in the white employee's face, and then a third white teammate entered the restroom and got in the white employee's face. Finally, the white employee decided that he didn't have any hassle left in him and he let Mr. Charles alone.[211]

• Figure skater Kristi Yamaguchi once skated a short program to "Doop Doop," by Dancelife Orchestra. In their short program, skaters are required to perform certain movements to demonstrate their technical skill. This created a problem for Kristi's choreographer, Sandra Bezic. "Doop Doop" is a funky song, danced to by hip chicks. What would any hip chick do during a traditional spiral, which is a required element in short programs? Ms. Bezic solved the problem by having Ms. Yamaguchi look bored during the spiral, holding her hand on her chin, tapping her cheek with a finger, and occasionally looking at her watch to see if it was time to stop the boring spiral. Ms. Bezic writes, "Competitive choreography is often about ways to do things differently within the confines of the rules."[212]

• At the San Francisco Giants' stadium, any home runs hit into the San Francisco Bay are probably presumed by most fans to be lost, but actually trained dogs rescue them. The dogs include Rio, a black Portuguese water dog, and several other dogs that are a part of

B.A.R.K., the Baseball Aquatic Retrieval Korps. B.A.R.K. is actually the brainchild of comedian Don Novello, aka Father Guido Sarducci. The aquatic-retrieval dogs sail on *The Good Ship Jollipup*, which is owned by an animal rescue organization called Pets in Need, and the dogs jump into the water and retrieve all the home-run balls hit there. Pets in Need auctions off the baseballs to fans, and the proceeds (and an added donation by the Giants) go toward finding good homes for pets in need.[213]

• *Tucson Weekly* columnist Tom Danehy has a *cuñado* [brother-in-law] named Jesse who entered the 111-mile El Tour de Tucson bicycle event a few years ago, although Tom says that this particular event is "usually reserved for the people who all look like they're Keira Knightley's cousins." In high school Jesse used to be a heavyweight wrestler — and has gained weight since then. Jesse trained for the event, he participated in the event, and he was so far behind the other cyclists — who had finished — that race officials jumped in front of his bike to tell him that the event was over. However, Jesse's goal was to finish the event, so he yelled, "I don't have any brakes!" and kept pedaling. The race officials jumped out of his way, and Jesse achieved his goal.[214]

• Managers and players have ways of letting umpires know that they want a game to be called on account of darkness or rain. Casey Stengel's team was ahead in the second game of a doubleheader, but the opposing team was threatening to take the lead, and Casey wanted the game called on account of darkness to ensure a win for his team. Therefore, he called for a relief pitcher — using Morse Code to signal with his flashlight. In another game, Herman "Germany" Schaefer thought that a game should be called on account of rain, so when he went to play in the outfield, he wore a raincoat over his uniform.[215]

• The great batter Ty Cobb was also respected as a base runner. When Connie Mack's Philadelphia Athletics and Mr. Cobb's Detroit Tigers were preparing for an important series, Mr. Mack went over strategy, discussing what to do against certain opposing players. At one point, he asked catcher Wally Shang, "Suppose that the Tigers were one run behind with Cobb on second base and you knew that he was going to steal on the next pitch. What would you do?" Mr. Shang replied, "I'd fake a throw to third, and then hold on to the ball and tag him as he came sliding into home plate."[216]

• Women's soccer coach Dan Tobias of the University of Arizona started his team practice every day at 6:45 a.m. It's not a punishment. Star player Brianna Caceres said, "He doesn't want us bummed out about the test we just took or distracted by other stuff. He wants us to have a good practice and then be energized for the academics and the rest of the day." Of course, soccer practice causes lots of sweat, so *Tucson Weekly* columnist Tom Danehy, who has an inquiring mind, had to ask her, "What about the funk?" Brianna answered, "Change of clothes, lots of body spray."[217]

• Once, when the Utah Jazz were slumping and losing, they had an away game against the Charlotte Hornets. Point guard John Stockton told big scorer Karl Malone before the game that he had listened to a Charlotte sports program, and a Charlotte player had said that Karl Malone was overrated as a player. This got Mr. Malone mad, and he scored 52 points that night, ending the Jazz' losing streak. After the game, Mr. Stockton confessed that no Charlotte player had disrespected Mr. Malone. Instead, Mr. Stockton had made the story up to motivate Mr. Malone.[218]

• Sports director Doug Wilson was faced with a problem—how to create a camera shot that would reveal the movement and the feel of skating. He solved the problem by putting a cameraperson in a wheelchair on the ice and having a skater push the wheelchair. By the way, ice skating Olympic gold medalist and announcer Dick Button is openly bald nowadays, but earlier he wore a toupee. Once, he was on the ice demonstrating a move for television when his toupee came off during a fast move. Like the trouper he is, he carried on.[219]

• For a while, major-league baseball player Kevin Mitchell had an unusual haircut: one with three strips shaved on the sides of his head. The three strips symbolically represented his first three hits in the major leagues. By the way, Mr. Mitchell is a problem-solver. While playing in the San Diego Padres' sometimes-chilly Candlestick Park, he used to put pepper between his toes on cold nights. Why? He explains, "When your feet sweat and the pepper dissolves, it makes your feet warm."[220]

• During a golf tournament, Walter Hagen hit his ball into a paper bag that had blown into a sand trap. After asking for a ruling, he was told that he couldn't take a free drop and that his options were to play the ball or to take a one-stroke penalty for an unplayable lie. Mr. Hagen responded by lighting a cigarette, taking a drag on it, then dropping the cigarette on the paper bag. The bag burned up, and Mr. Hagen played the lie.[221]

• In the 18th century, the boxing ring was at ground level, and fans became so excited that sometimes they would jump into the ring and start fighting. To solve that problem, boxing promoter Jack Broughton added ropes to the ring and raised the ring six feet from the ground. His innovations are still in effect today.[222]

• The late Chuck Daley used to coach the Detroit Pistons. Often, he would take players out of the game — players who objected vociferously at being taken out of the game. When a reporter asked him how he handled such situations, Mr. Daley said, "I'm over 70. I don't always hear so good."[223]

• Figure-skating choreographer Sandra Bezic enjoys being on the ice. Whenever she works with pairs team Barbara Underhill and Paul Martini and feels like getting a figure-skating "fix," she asks Mr. Martini to perform the movement known as a death spiral with her.[224]

• In 1993 at the Hong Kong Open, rain washed out the first two rounds. Greg Norman wanted to practice despite the rain, so he hit golf balls through an open window in his hotel residence into the harbor. And yes, he won the Hong Kong Open.[225]

Records

• When Walter Payton broke the NFL record, held by Jim Brown, for most games rushing 100 yards or more, he was asked who he would like to see break his record. He replied, "I don't care who breaks my record once I retire — as long as it's my son."[226]

• When Gertrude Ederle became the first woman to swim across the English Channel in 1926 (knocking two hours off the men's record), reporters asked her how she felt as she walked onto shore. She replied, "Wet."[227]

Scouts

• Roy Cullenbine was an outfielder long ago. When he was still playing bush-league baseball, a sportswriter told him to play especially well that day because two scouts were in the stands and if he played well, they would want to see him after the game. Mr. Cullenbine did play well, making four hits and several spectacular catches. Sure enough, after the game, two scouts were waiting to meet him — they were Boy Scouts.[228]

• In 1912, baseball player Casey Stengel was scouted on a day on which he could do little right. He tried to steal twice — and was thrown out each time. He made a spectacular catch — and threw the ball to the wrong base. He reached base once — and found himself sharing the base with a teammate. The scout reported, "Stengel can run, throw, and hit. He's the most promising I've ever seen — from the neck down."[229]

Signs

• Major-league baseball pitcher Bob Gibson had a sense of humor. After he broke his leg, he got tired of answering the same questions over and over from sportswriters; therefore, after the cast came off his leg, he wore a sign around his neck with the answers to the questions that sportswriters kept asking him: "1. Yes, it's off! 2. No, it doesn't hurt. 3. I'm not supposed to walk on it for a week. 4. I don't know how much longer. 5. Ask Doc Bauman. 6. Ask Doc Middleman." In addition, he once drew eyes on his bat so it could "see" the ball and he would get more hits. It must have worked: In his career, he achieved a grand total of 24 home runs in regular-season play. His last major-league home run was a grand slam against the Mets.[230]

• Early in his career, African-American tennis great Arthur Ashe played at a club that had this sign out front: "Whites Only." Fortunately, the sign meant that white tails were to be worn at the club that night, but Mr. Ashe did not feel good looking at the sign.[231]

• For 18 years, Gary McCord did not have a single win on the PGA Tour. Therefore, he acquired his own vanity license plate: NO WINS. Finally, in 1991, he won on the Hogan Tour. Because of the win, he added an asterisk to his license plate.[232]

Superstitions

• Many hitters have strange beliefs about their bats. In the mid-1950s, Forrest "Spook" Jacobs used to squirt eye drops on his bat because he thought his hitting prowess improved when he used a "seeing-eye" bat. In the early 1900s, John "Chief" Meyers would not allow his fellow players to use his bats because he believed that each bat was capable of making only 100 hits. One of Meyers' teammates, Benny Kauff, rested his bats whenever he felt that they were tired.[233]

• Athletes frequently have odd superstitions and do odd things that they feel bring them good luck. Sarah Hughes, who won a gold medal in ladies' figure skating at the 2002 Winter Olympics, always slept in a Peggy Fleming T-shirt before important competitions. Ms. Fleming even sent her one with this note: "P.F.'s PJs."[234]

Training

• Veronica Walker, the sister of NBA great Herschel Walker, was a track star. When Herschel was young, he wanted to beat her in a race, but he was pudgy and he could not beat her. Getting tired of losing all the time, he asked Tom Jordan, the coach of the Johnson County (Georgia) track and field team, what he had to do to beat her. Coach Jordan, who was full of common sense, told him, "Do pushups. Do situps. Run sprints." Herschel worked hard at pushups, situps, and sprints, and after much, much work, he beat his sister in a race. Immediately, he set a new goal — he tried to beat a pet horse in a race. His mother, who was full of common sense, told him, "Herschel, you can't outrun a horse." She was right. He tried a beat a pet horse in a race, but he lost. His father was another person who was full of common sense. Herschel and his siblings wanted to practice their jumping, and they talked about jumping over their father's car. Their father quickly put an end to such talk: "You fool kids, that's my car! You'll get hurt. I've got no money to pay for hospitals." All of Herschel's hard work paid off. In high school, he did not lift weights, but when his high school got some new weightlifting equipment, he decided to give it a try. He lifted 250 pounds a few times, and then he told his coach, "Coach, 250 pounds isn't heavy."[235]

• Triathlete Heather Hedrick takes her sport seriously, and so do the other athletes she hangs out with. One advantage of having fellow athletes as her friends is that everyone is training. According to Ms. Hedrick, "I'm never the party pooper. Everyone else goes home at 10 p.m., too."[236]

Umpires

• It doesn't pay to try to win an argument with an umpire. Detroit Tiger Bobby Veach hit a ball over the third-base line and took off running before umpire Tommy Connolly ruled whether it was fair or foul. Mr. Veach was standing on second base when Umpire Connolly yelled at him, "Foul ball. You'll have to hit another." Mr. Veach grumbled, but left second base to return to the batter's box. When the inning was over, he ran to the third-base line where his ball had dropped, then came running back to Umpire Connolly to report, "That ball was fair, Tommy. It landed right on the foul line, and there's a mark in the lime where it landed. You can see it plainly." Umpire Connolly smiled and said, "I'll tell you what I'll do. You just run out and bring that foul line to me, and I'll have a look at it!"[237]

• Sometimes, umpires get blamed for what other umpires do. A minor-league umpire named Kerin worked a game that upset some home fans who abused him mightily, and Mr. Kerin challenged any fan who wanted to fight him to see him after the game. The next day, Harry "Steamboat" Johnson came in to umpire, and fans yelled things at him like, "Kerin, you better get the cops to look after you when this game is over, because we are after you and mean business." Not until halfway through the game did the fans realize that Steamboat was not Mr. Kerin. In telling this story in his autobiography, *Standing the Gaff*, Steamboat marvels about fans, "And still they try to call close plays from where they sit!"[238]

• Umpire Tom Gorman once had his leg broken when Al Oliver and Paul Popovich collided at first base, blindsiding him. He was lying on the ground in pain when Leo Durocher came over and asked for a ruling, screaming, "What is he? Safe or out? Safe or out?" Although he was in great pain, Mr. Gorman managed to joke, "He's out — he had the wrong foot on base." In the next inning, when Mr. Gorman was in the hospital, Mr. Durocher thought about the answer he had been given, and he started screaming again: "What did Gorman mean — 'wrong foot'? There's no 'right' foot." But the other umpires answered, "Too late, Leo. You'll have to ask Tom."[239]

• Minor-league umpires Don Denkinger and Ron Luciano were together when they received a telephone call from the American League. The caller asked to speak to Mr. Denkinger and told him to be happy for Mr. Luciano because he was going to be offered a contract to be an umpire in the major leagues. Then the caller asked to speak to Mr. Luciano and told him to be happy for Mr. Denkinger because he was going to be offered a contract to be an umpire in the major leagues. That's how Mr. Denkinger and Mr. Luciano learned that they were major-league umpires.[240]

War

• Pelé was such an internationally acclaimed soccer star that even war stopped for him. When Nigeria and Biafra were at war with each other, Pelé needed to go from Nigeria to Biafra so that he could play soccer. The war stopped so that Pelé could travel safely, and the war stayed stopped until the two opposing armies could escort Pelé safely out of the war zone. This is not bad for someone whose father taught him how to play soccer as a small child by using a bundle of rags tied up into a ball. By the way, Pelé's real name is Edson Arantes do Nascimento — Pelé is a nickname that means "The Black Pearl."[241]

• During World War II, baseball announcers weren't allowed to comment about the weather because of fear that Japanese radio monitors might pick up on the information and get some military advantage out of it. Once, retired pitcher Dizzy Dean was broadcasting a game when it was stopped because of a rainstorm. He told his radio audience, "Folks, the game has been called temporarily. I ain't allowed to tell you why, but if you're curious, just stick your head out the window."[242]

• During the Vietnam War, Arthur Ashe played some tennis in Saigon for the USAmerican troops. At one point, someone in the car he was riding in rolled down the window because of the heat, but a soldier in the car said, "Roll that window up. Tell you what, you leave a window down and sometimes a little guy will ride by on a bike and drop a grenade in your lap."[243]

Work

• Major-league umpire Bill Klem must have loved his job. Early in his career, he worked as a bartender and did some umpiring on the side. Once, a friend told him about an umpiring job — a doubleheader — in Providence, Rhode Island, 50 miles away. Mr. Klem was willing to work it, and so the two men rode on a tandem bicycle to Providence, worked the two games, and then rode the bicycle back home, just in time for Mr. Klem to go to his bartending job. For working the doubleheader, Mr. Klem earned $10, and afterward, he said to himself, "Why, this is easy." Fellow umpire Jocko Conlan says, "Ride a bike 100 miles, work a doubleheader, earn ten bucks, and call it easy. He had to be a born umpire."[244]

• Vince Lombardi and his staff were hard workers. When the Green Bay Packers won the 1965 National Football League championship by defeating the Cleveland Browns, 23-12, sportswriters asked Mr. Lombardi about his vacation plans. He replied, "I've got a meeting scheduled with my coaching staff. We're going to start to lay out plans for 1966. We're starting work tomorrow morning at 9 a.m." This doesn't mean that Mr. Lombardi had absolutely no plans for a vacation. He told the reporters, "Maybe I'll take a week off in February. Maybe two weeks."[245]

• Seattle Mariners first baseman Edgar Martinez was a role model for shortstop Alex Rodriguez. One day, Alex took batting practice and left at 2 p.m. However, he discovered that he had left his cell phone behind. Returning to the clubhouse at 6 p.m. to pick it up, he discovered Mr. Martinez still taking batting practice. Surprised that this two-time batting champion was still hard at work, Alex asked, "Edgar, what are you still doing here?" Mr. Martinez replied, "I have to hit. I have to work." Quickly, Mr. Rodriguez decided to emulate Mr. Martinez.[246]

• A young, green umpire told minor-league umpire Harry "Steamboat" Johnson, "I'm a plate umpire," and Steamboat said, "OK." He let the young umpire work behind home plate, wearing the bulky chest protector in the hot summer sun, until the young umpire asked him, "Mr. Johnson, aren't I ever going to work the bases?" Steamboat, who had been enjoying not wearing all the bulky home umpire gear, replied, "I thought you said you were a plate umpire."[247]

• Muhammad Ali owned a lot of fancy cars, and he hired a chauffeur; however, he enjoyed driving his cars so much that often his chauffeur sat in the back seat while Mr. Ali drove. Occasionally, Mr. Ali would joke that he had taken a part-time job as a chauffeur, and he would point to the real chauffeur in the back seat and say, "That's the white boss in the back."[248]

World Series

• When pitcher Greg Maddux became a free agent after the 1992 season, he had a chance to sign with the New York Yankees; however, he signed with the Atlanta Braves although they offered him $6 million less than the Yankees. He had two main reasons for this: 1) He and his wife, Kathy, felt that Atlanta would be a better place to raise their children, and 2) he felt that he had a better chance of winning a World Series with the Braves. These two considerations were more important than the money. Playing for the Braves worked out well for Mr. Maddox; in 1995, the Braves won the World Series.[249]

• Brooklyn Dodger Gil Hodges suffered a horrible hitting slump in the 1952 World Series, getting no hits at all in 21 at-bats. His slump continued during the first part of the 1953 season. A priest (and Dodger fan) urged his congregation to do two things: keep God's commandments and pray for Gil Hodges. The prayers worked. He started to hit again, he had a very good 1953 season, he had a very good 1953 World Series although the Dodgers lost, and he helped the Dodgers win the 1955 World Series.[250]

Appendix A: Bibliography

Aaseng, Nathan. *Sports Great David Robinson*. Berkeley Heights, NJ: Enslow Publishers, Inc., 1998.

Aaseng, Nathan. *Sports Great John Stockton*. Springfield, NJ: Enslow Publishers, Inc., 1995.

Ashby, R.S. *Sarah Hughes: America's Sweetheart*. New York: Avon Books, 2002.

Barich, Bill. *The Sporting Life: Horses, Boxers, Rivers, and a Soviet Ballclub*. New York: The Lyons Press, 1999.

Benagh, Jim. *Sports Great Herschel Walker*. Hillside, NJ: Enslow Publishers, Inc., 1990.

Bezic, Sandra. *The Passion to Skate: An Intimate View of Figure Skating*. With David Hayes. Atlanta, GA: Turner Publishing, Inc., 1996.

Bortstein, Larry. *After Olympic Glory: The Lives of Ten Outstanding Medalists*. New York: Frederick Warne, 1978.

Burchard, S.H. *Pelé*. New York: Harcourt Brace Jovanovich, Publishers, 1976.

Campbell, Jim. *The Importance of Joe Louis*. San Diego, CA: Lucent, 1997.

Carlson, Stan W. *Baseball Banter: Gems of the Baseball Diamond*. Minneapolis, MN: The Author, 1940.

Claus, S. *Holiday Cheer for the 19th Hole*. With help from Russ Edwards and Jack Kreismer. Saddle River, NJ: Red-Letter Press, 2003.

Clower, Jerry. *Ain't God Good!* Waco, TX: Word Books, Publisher, 1975.

Clower, Jerry. *Let the Hammer Down!* With Gerry Wood. Waco, TX: Word Books, Publisher, 1979.

Cohen, Joel. *Odd Moments in Baseball*. New York: Scholastic, Inc., 2000.

Cohen, Sasha. *Fire on Ice: Autobiography of a Champion Figure Skater*. With Amanda Maciel. New York: HarperCollins Publishers, 2005.

Comaneci, Nadia. *Letters to a Young Gymnast*. New York: Basic Books, 2004.

Conlan, Jocko, and Robert W. Creamer. *Jocko*. Lincoln, NE: University of Nebraska Press, 1997.

Conner, Bart. *Winning the Gold*. With Coach Paul Ziert. New York: Warner Books, Inc., 1985.

Cranston, Toller. *Zero Tollerance*. With Martha Lowder Kimball. Toronto, Canada: McClelland and Stewart, Inc., 1997.

Crum, Jimmy, and Carole Gerber. *How About That! Jimmy Crum: Fifty Years of Cliffhangers and Barn-Burners*. Columbus, OH: Fine Line Graphics, 1993.

Crutcher, Chris. *King of the Mild Frontier*. New York: Greenwillow Books, 2003.

Davis, Mac. *100 Greatest Sports Feats*. New York: Grosset and Dunlap, Publishers, 1964.

Davis, Mac. *Strange and Incredible Sports Happenings*. New York: Grosset and Dunlap, Publishers, 1975.

Deane, Bill. *Bob Gibson*. New York: Chelsea House Publishers, 1994.

DeVos, Dick. *Rediscovering American Values: The Foundations of Our Freedom in the 21st Century*. New York: The Penguin Group, 1997.

Dickey, Glenn. *Sports Great Kevin Mitchell*. Hillside, NJ: Enslow Publishers, Inc., 1993.

Donohue, Shiobhan. *Kristi Yamaguchi: Artist on Ice*. Minneapolis, MN: Lerner Publications Company, 1994.

Eckhouse, Morris. *Bob Feller*. New York: Chelsea House Publishers, 1990.

Erskine, Carl. *Carl Erskine's Tales from the Dodger Dugout*. Champaigne, IL: Sports Publishing Inc., 2000.

Farran, Christopher. *Dogs on the Job! True Stories of Phenomenal Dogs*. New York: Avon Books, 2003.

Fecher, Msgr. Vincent. *"The Lord and I": Vignettes from the Life of a Parish Priest*. New York: Alba House, 1990.

Fehr, Kristin Smith. *Monica Seles: Returning Champion*. Minneapolis, MN: Lerner Publications Company, 1997.

Feinstein, Stephen. *The 1970s: From Watergate to Disco*. Berkeley Heights, NJ: Enslow Publications, Inc., 2000.

Fleming, Peggy. *The Long Program*. With Peter Kaminsky. New York: Pocket Books, 1999.

Ford, Carin T. *Muhammad Ali: "I Am the Greatest."* Berkeley Heights, NJ: Enslow Publishers, Inc., 2006.

Garagiola, Joe. *It's Anybody's Ballgame*. New York: Jove Books, 1988.

Gardner, Robert, and Dennis Shortelle. *The Forgotten Players: The Story of Black Baseball in America*. New York: Walker and Company, 1993.

Garner, Joe. *Stay Tuned: Television's Unforgettable Moments*. Kansas City, MO: Andrews McMeel Publishing, 2002.

Gikow, Louise A. *Extreme Sports*. New York: Children's Press, 2004.

Gilbert, Thomas W. *Roberto Clemente*. New York: Chelsea House Publishers, 1991.

Gottesman, Jane. *Game Face: What Does A Female Athlete Look Like?* New York: Random House, 2001.

Green, Septima. *Top 10 Women Gymnasts*. Berkeley Heights, NJ: Enslow Publications, Inc., 1999.

Greenberg, Keith Elliot. *Pro Wrestling: From Carnivals to Cable TV*. Minneapolis, MN: Lerner Publications Company, 2000.

Greenberg, Paul. *Resonant Lives: 60 Figures of Consequence*. Washington, D.C.: Ethics and Public Policy Center, 1993.

Greenberg, Steve, and Dale Ratermann. *I Remember Woody: Recollections of the Man They Called Coach Hayes*. Indianapolis, IN: Masters Press, 1997.

Greenspan, Bud. *100 Greatest Moments in Olympic History*. Los Angeles, CA: General Publishing Group, Inc., 1995.

Gutman, Bill. *More Modern Women Superstars*. New York: Dodd, Mead and Company, 1979.

Gutman, Bill. *Tara Lipinski: Queen of the Ice*. Brookfield, CT: The Millbrook Press, 1999.

Gutman, Dan. *Gymnastics: The Trials, the Triumphs, the Truth*. New York: Puffin Books, 1996.

Haney, Lynn. *The Lady is a Jock*. New York: Dodd, Mead, and Company, 1973.

Haney, Lynn. *Perfect Balance: The Story of an Elite Gymnast*. New York: G.P. Putnam's Sons, 1979.

Harrington, Denis J. *Sports Great Jim Kelly*. Springfield, NJ: Enslow Publishers, Inc., 1996.

Harrington, Denis J. *Top 10 Women's Tennis Players*. Springfield, NJ: Enslow Publications, Inc., 1995.

Haskins, James. *Babe Ruth and Hank Aaron: The Home Run Kings*. New York: Lothrop, Lee & Shepard Company, 1974.

Haskins, James. *Sports Great Magic Johnson*. Hillside, NJ: Enslow Publishers, Inc., 1992.

Hill, Christine M. *Ten Terrific Authors for Teens*. Berkeley Heights, NJ: Enslow Publications, Inc., 2000.

Hughes, Morgan E. *Mario Lemieux: Beating the Odds*. Minneapolis, MN: Lerner Publications Company, 1996.

Jacobsen, Peter. *Embedded Balls*. With Jack Sheehan. New York: G.P. Putnam's Sons, 2005.

Jacobson, Steve. *Carrying Jackie's Torch: The Players Who Integrated Baseball — and America*. Chicago, IL: Lawrence Hill Books, 2007.

Jenkins, Ron. *Acrobats of the Soul*. New York: Theatre Communications Group, Inc., 1988.

Johnson, Harry "Steamboat." *Standing the Gaff: The Life and Hard Times of a Minor League Umpire*. Introduction to the Bison Book edition by Larry R. Gerlach. Lincoln, NE: University of Nebraska Press, 1994.

Karolyi, Bela, and Nancy Ann Richardson. *Feel No Fear: The Power, Passion, and Politics of a Life in Gymnastics*. New York: Hyperion, 1994.

Katella-Cofrancesco, Kathy. *Economic Causes*. Brookfield, CT: Twenty-First Century Books, 1998.

Kavanagh, Jack. *Sports Great Larry Bird*. Hillside, NJ: Enslow Publishers, Inc., 1992.

Kavanagh, Jack. *Sports Great Patrick Ewing*. Hillside, NJ: Enslow Publishers, Inc., 1992.

Kindred, Dave. *Heroes, Fools, and Other Dreamers: A Sportswriter's Gallery of Extraordinary People*. Atlanta, GA: Longstreet Press, 1988.

King, Chuck. *The Funniest Thing I've Ever Seen: More Than 100 Crazy Stories from Minor League Baseball*. Morristown, NC: Lulu Press, 2006.

Knapp, Ron. *Sports Great Bo Jackson*. Hillside, NJ: Enslow Publications, Inc., 1990.

Knapp, Ron. *Sports Great Bobby Bonilla*. Springfield, NJ: Enslow Publishers, Inc., 1993.

Krull, Kathleen. *Lives of the Athletes: Thrills, Spills (And What the Neighbors Thought)*. San Diego, CA: Harcourt Brace and Company, 1997.

Lace, William W. *Sports Great Nolan Ryan*. Hillside, NJ: Enslow Publishers, Inc., 1993.

Laskas, Jeanne Marie. *We Remember: Women Born at the Turn of the Century Tell the Stories of Their Lives*. Photographs by Lynn Johnson. New York: William Morrow and Company, 1999.

Layden, Joe. *Kobe: The Story of the NBA's Rising Young Star*. New York: HarperPaperbacks, 1998.

Lemmon, Chris. *A Twist of Lemmon: A Tribute to My Father*. Chapel Hill, NC: Algonquin Books of Chapel Hill, 2006.

Lindop, Laurie. *Athletes*. New York: Twenty-First Century Books, 1996.

Linkletter, Art. *I Wish I'd Said That! My Favorite Ad-Libs of All Time*. Garden City, NY: Doubleday & Co., Inc., 1968.

Lipsyte, Robert. *Assignment: Sports*. New York: Harper & Row, Publishers, 1984.

Long, Barbara. *Jim Thorpe: Legendary Athlete*. Springfield, NJ: Enslow Publications, Inc., 1997.

Long, Shepard. *Carl Yastrzemski*. New York: Chelsea House Publishers, 1993.

Lovitt, Chip. *American Gymnasts: Gold Medal Dreams*. New York: Pocket Books, 2000.

Macnow, Glen. *Sports Great Alex Rodriguez*. Berkeley Heights, NJ, 2002.

Macnow, Glen. *Sports Great Cal Ripken, Jr.* Hillside, NJ: Enslow Publishers, Inc., 1993.

Macht, Norman L. *Babe Ruth*. New York: Chelsea House Publishers, 1991.

Margolies, Jacob. *The Negro Leagues: The Story of Black Baseball*. New York: Franklin Watts, 1993.

Marx, Arthur. *Son of Groucho*. New York: David McKay Company, Inc., 1972.

Masin, Herman L. *For Laughing Out Loud: Football's Funniest Stories*. New York: Scholastic Book Services, 1954.

Masin, Herman L. *The Funniest Moments in Sports*. New York: M. Evans and Company, 1974.

Molen, Sam. *Take 2 and Hit to Right*. Philadelphia, PA: Dorrance and Company, 1959.

Molen, Sam. *They Make Me Laugh*. Philadelphia, PA: Dorrance and Company, 1947.

Morgan, Terri. *Gabrielle Reece: Volleyball's Model Athlete*. Minneapolis, MN: Lerner Publications Company, 1999.

Murray, Jim. *The Best of Jim Murray*. Garden City, NY: Doubleday & Company, Inc., 1965.

Olney, Ross R. *Lyn St. James: Driven to Be First*. Minneapolis, MN: Lerner Publications Company, 1997.

Olsen, Marilyn. *Women Who Risk: Profiles of Women in Extreme Sports*. New York: Hatherleigh Press, 2001.

Packard, Mary. *Against the Odds: A Chapter Book*. New York: Children's Press, 2004.

Pellowski, Michael J. *Baseball's Funniest People*. New York: Sterling Publishing Co., 1997.

Quiner, Krista. *Dominique Moceanu: A Gymnastics Sensation*. East Hanover, NJ: The Bradford Book Company, 1997.

Rappoport, Ken, and Barry Wilner. *Girls Rule! The Glory and Spirit of Women in Sports*. Kansas City, MO: Andrews McMeel Publishing, 2000.

Rappoport, Ken, and Barry Wilner. *Villains: The Bad Boys and Girls of Sport*. Atlanta, GA: Lionheart Books, Ltd., 2000.

Riley, James A. *The Negro Leagues*. Philadelphia, PA: Chelsea House Publishers, 1997.

Rockwell, Bart. *World's Strangest Football Stories*. Mahwah, NJ: Watermill Press, 1993.

Rockwell, Bart. *World's Strangest Hockey Stories*. Mahwah, NJ: Watermill Press, 1993.

Rosen, Michael J., editor. *Dog People: Writers and Artists on Canine Companionship*. New York: Artisan, 1995.

Russell, Bill. *Red and Me: My Coach, My Lifelong Friend*. With Alan Steinberg. New York: HarperCollins Publishers, 2009.

Russell, Fred, teller. *Funny Thing About Sports*. Nashville, TN: The McQuiddy Press, 1948.

Russell, Fred. *I'll Go Quietly*. Nashville, TN: The McQuiddy Press, 1944.

Savage, Jeff. *Julie Foudy: Soccer Superstar*. Minneapolis, MN: Lerner Publications Company, 1999.

Savage, Jeff. *Julie Krone: Unstoppable Jockey*. Minneapolis, MN: Lerner Publications Company, 1996.

Schafer, Kermit. *Best of Bloopers*. New York: Avenel Books, 1973.

Schlegel, Elfi, and Claire Ross Dunn. *The Gymnastics Book: The Young Performer's Guide to Gymnastics*. Buffalo, NY: Firefly Books, Inc., 2001.

Schoor, Gene. *Football's Greatest Coach: Vince Lombardi*. New York: Pocket Books, 1975.

Silver, Eric. *The Book of the Just: The Unsung Heroes Who Rescued Jews from Hitler*. New York: Grove Press, 1992.

Silverstein, Herma. *Mary Lou Retton and the New Gymnasts*. New York: Franklin Watts, 1985.

Skipper, John C. *Umpires: Classic Baseball Stories from the Men Who Made the Calls*. Jefferson, NC, and London: McFarland and Company, Inc., Publishers, 1997.

Smith, Beverley. *Talking Figure Skating*. Toronto, Ontario, Canada: McClelland & Stewart, Inc., 1997.

Smith, Elson. *The Blooper Man: The Rip Sewell Story*. Bellevue, PA: J. Pohl Associates, 1981.

Smith, H. Allen. *The Compleat Practical Joker*. Garden City, NY: Doubleday and Company, Inc., 1953.

Smith, H. Allen. *How to Write Without Knowing Nothing*. Boston, MA: Little, Brown, and Company, 1961.

Snead, Sam. *The Game I Love: Wisdom, Insight, and Instruction from Golf's Greatest Player*. With Fran Pirozzolo. New York: Ballantine Books, 1997.

Sobol, Donald J. *Encyclopedia Brown's Book of Wacky Sports*. New York: William Morrow and Company, 1984.

Steenkamer, Paul. *Sports Great Donovan McNabb*. Berkeley Heights, NJ: Enslow Publishers, Inc., 2003.

Straus, Hal, editor. *Gymnastics Guide*. Mountain View, CA: World Publications, 1978.

Sufrin, Mark. *Payton*. New York: Charles Scribner's Sons, 1988.

Thomas, Kurt, and Kent Hannon. *Kurt Thomas on Gymnastics*. New York: Simon and Schuster, 1980.

Thornley, Stew. *Sports Great Greg Maddux*. Berkeley Heights, NJ: Enslow Publishers, Inc., 1997.

Torres, John A. *Home-Run Hitters: Heroes of the Four Home-Run Game*. New York: Macmillan Books for Young Readers, 1995.

Torres, John Albert, and Michael John Sullivan. *Sports Great Darryl Strawberry*. Hillside, NJ: Enslow Publishers, Inc., 1990.

Towle, Mike. *I Remember Arthur Ashe*. Nashville, TN: Cumberland House, 2001.

Towle, Mike. *I Remember Walter Payton*. Nashville, TN: Cumberland House, 2000.

Tuttle, Dennis R. *Albert Belle*. Philadelphia, PA: Chelsea House Publishers, n.d.

Wade, Don. *"And Then Arnie Told Chi Chi ...."* Chicago, IL: Contemporary Books, 1993.

Wilner, Barry. *Scott Hamilton: Star Figure Skater*. Berkeley Heights, NJ: Enslow Publications, Inc., 1999.

Wood, Rob, editor. *It's All in the Game: Funny Happenings for Those Who Love Sports*. Kansas City, MO. Hallmark Cards, Inc., 1976.

Wulffson, Don L. *When Human Heads Were Footballs*. New York: Aladdin Books, 1998.

Zack, Bill. *Chipper Jones*. Philadelphia, PA: Chelsea House Publishers, 1999.

Appendix B: About the Author

It was a dark and stormy night. Suddenly a cry rang out, and on a hot summer night in 1954, Josephine, wife of Carl Bruce, gave birth to a boy — me. Unfortunately, this young married couple allowed Reuben Saturday, Josephine's brother, to name their first-born. Reuben, aka "The Joker," decided that Bruce was a nice name, so he decided to name me Bruce Bruce. I have gone by my middle name — David — ever since.

Being named Bruce David Bruce hasn't been all bad. Bank tellers remember me very quickly, so I don't often have to show an ID. It can be fun in charades, also. When I was a counselor as a teenager at Camp Echoing Hills in Warsaw, Ohio, a fellow counselor gave the signs for "sounds like" and "two words," then she pointed to a bruise on her leg twice. Bruise Bruise? Oh yeah, Bruce Bruce is the answer!

Uncle Reuben, by the way, gave me a haircut when I was in kindergarten. He cut my hair short and shaved a small bald spot on the back of my head. My mother wouldn't let me go to school until the bald spot grew out again.

Of all my brothers and sisters (six in all), I am the only transplant to Athens, Ohio. I was born in Newark, Ohio, and have lived all around Southeastern Ohio. However, I moved to Athens to go to Ohio University and have never left.

At Ohio U, I never could make up my mind whether to major in English or Philosophy, so I got a bachelor's degree with a double major in both areas, then I added a Master of Arts degree in English and a Master of Arts degree in Philosophy. Yes, I have my MAMA degree.

Currently, and for a long time to come (I eat fruits and veggies), I am spending my retirement writing books such as *Nadia Comaneci: Perfect 10*, *The Funniest People in Comedy*, *Homer's* Iliad: *A Retelling in Prose*, and *William Shakespeare's* Hamlet: *A Retelling in Prose.*

If all goes well, I will publish one or two books a year for the rest of my life. (On the other hand, a good way to make God laugh is to tell Her your plans.)

Appendix C: Some Books by David Bruce

Anecdote Collections

250 Anecdotes About Opera

250 Anecdotes About Religion

250 Anecdotes About Religion: Volume 2

250 Music Anecdotes

Be a Work of Art: 250 Anecdotes and Stories

The Coolest People in Art: 250 Anecdotes

The Coolest People in the Arts: 250 Anecdotes

The Coolest People in Books: 250 Anecdotes

The Coolest People in Comedy: 250 Anecdotes

Create, Then Take a Break: 250 Anecdotes

Don't Fear the Reaper: 250 Anecdotes

The Funniest People in Art: 250 Anecdotes

The Funniest People in Books: 250 Anecdotes

The Funniest People in Books, Volume 2: 250 Anecdotes

The Funniest People in Books, Volume 3: 250 Anecdotes

The Funniest People in Comedy: 250 Anecdotes

The Funniest People in Dance: 250 Anecdotes

The Funniest People in Families: 250 Anecdotes

The Funniest People in Families, Volume 2: 250 Anecdotes

The Funniest People in Families, Volume 3: 250 Anecdotes

The Funniest People in Families, Volume 4: 250 Anecdotes

The Funniest People in Families, Volume 5: 250 Anecdotes

The Funniest People in Families, Volume 6: 250 Anecdotes

The Funniest People in Movies: 250 Anecdotes

The Funniest People in Music: 250 Anecdotes

The Funniest People in Music, Volume 2: 250 Anecdotes

The Funniest People in Music, Volume 3: 250 Anecdotes

The Funniest People in Neighborhoods: 250 Anecdotes

The Funniest People in Relationships: 250 Anecdotes

The Funniest People in Sports: 250 Anecdotes

The Funniest People in Sports, Volume 2: 250 Anecdotes

The Funniest People in Television and Radio: 250 Anecdotes

The Funniest People in Theater: 250 Anecdotes

The Funniest People Who Live Life: 250 Anecdotes
The Funniest People Who Live Life, Volume 2: 250 Anecdotes
The Kindest People Who Do Good Deeds, Volume 1: 250 Anecdotes
The Kindest People Who Do Good Deeds, Volume 2: 250 Anecdotes
Maximum Cool: 250 Anecdotes
The Most Interesting People in Movies: 250 Anecdotes
The Most Interesting People in Politics and History: 250 Anecdotes
The Most Interesting People in Politics and History, Volume 2: 250 Anecdotes
The Most Interesting People in Politics and History, Volume 3: 250 Anecdotes
The Most Interesting People in Religion: 250 Anecdotes
The Most Interesting People in Sports: 250 Anecdotes
The Most Interesting People Who Live Life: 250 Anecdotes
The Most Interesting People Who Live Life, Volume 2: 250 Anecdotes
Reality is Fabulous: 250 Anecdotes and Stories
Resist Psychic Death: 250 Anecdotes
Seize the Day: 250 Anecdotes and Stories

[1]Source: Joe Garner, *Stay Tuned: Television's Unforgettable Moments*, pp. 138-139.

[2]Source: Denis J. Harrington, *Top 10 Women's Tennis Players*, pp. 4, 30-33. Also: Stephen Feinstein, *The 1970s: From Watergate to Disco*, p. 27.

[3]Source: Jeanne Marie Laskas, *We Remember*, p. 99.

[4]Source: Keith Elliot Greenberg, *Pro Wrestling: From Carnivals to Cable TV*, p. 57.

[5]Source: Rob Wood, editor, *It's All in the Game: Funny Happenings for Those Who Love Sports*, p. 7.

[6] Source: Peter Jacobsen, *Embedded Balls*, pp. 143-144.

[7]Source: Sam Snead, *The Game I Love*, p. 128.

[8] Source: Bud Greenspan, *100 Greatest Moments in Olympic History*, pp. 24-25.

[9]Source: Bart Conner, *Winning the Gold*, pp. 20-21, 89.

[10]Source: Barry Wilner, *Scott Hamilton: Star Figure Skater*, p. 25.

[11] Source: Mike Towle, *I Remember Walter Payton*, pp. 176-177.

[12] Source: Peter Jacobsen, *Embedded Balls*, pp. 204-205.

[13] Source: Jack Kavanagh, *Sports Great Patrick Ewing*, pp. 19, 22-23.

[14]Source: Fred Russell, *I'll Go Quietly*, p. 16.

[15] Source: Morris Eckhouse, *Bob Feller*, p. 14.

[16]Source: Beverley Smith, *Talking Figure Skating*, p. 225, 229-230.

[17]Source: Kristin Smith Fehr, *Monica Seles: Returning Champion*, pp. 30-31.

[18]Source: Jacob Margolies, *The Negro Leagues: The Story of Black Baseball*, p. 44.

[19]Source: Joe Garagiola, *It's Anybody's Ballgame*, p. 63.

[20] Source: Robert Gardner and Dennis Shortelle, *The Forgotten Players: The Story of Black Baseball in America*, p. 66.

[21] Source: Paul Greenberg, *Resonant Lives: 60 Figures of Consequence*, pp. 40-42.

[22] Source: Bill Barich, *The Sporting Life*, pp. 62-63.

[23]Source: Arthur Marx, *Son of Groucho*, p. 50.

[24]Source: Dan Gutman, *Gymnastics: The Trials, the Triumphs, the Truth*, p. 15.

[25] Source: Bill Zack, *Chipper Jones*, pp. 15-17, 51.

[26] Source: Denis J. Harrington, *Sports Great Jim Kelly*, pp. 13-14.

[27] Source: Nadia Comaneci, *Letters to a Young Gymnast*, p. 56.

[28] Source: Dick DeVos, *Rediscovering American Values*, p. 24.

[29] Source: Dennis R. Tuttle, *Albert Belle*, p. 16.

[30] Source: Barry Wilner, *Scott Hamilton: Star Figure Skater*, p. 22.

[31] Source: Kristin Smith Fehr, *Monica Seles: Returning Champion*, pp. 13-14.

[32] Source: Krista Quiner, *Dominique Moceanu: A Gymnastics Sensation*, p. 20.

[33] Source: Lynn Haney, *Perfect Balance*, p. 47.

[34] Source: Christine M. Hill, *Ten Terrific Authors for Teens*, p. 46.

[35] Source: Jeff Savage, *Julie Foudy: Soccer Superstar*, p. 18.

[36] Source: Simon Hattenstone, "I'm ashamed of so many things I've done." *The Guardian*. 21 March 2009 <http://www.guardian.co.uk/sport/2009/mar/21/mike-tyson-interview-boxing>.

[37] Source: Sam Snead, *The Game I Love*, p. 129.

[38] Source: Jack Kavanagh, *Sports Great Larry Bird*, pp. 17-18.

[39] Source: Camilla Mortensen, "It's Good to Be the Queen: Rodeo royalty in rural Oregon." *Eugene Weekly*. 27 March 2008 <http://eugeneweekly.com/2008/03/27/coverstory.htmlPER>.

[40] Source: Toller Cranston, *Zero Tollerance*, pp. 223-225.

[41] Source: Jeff Savage, *Julie Krone: Unstoppable Jockey*, p. 38.

[42] Source: Lynn Haney, *The Lady is a Jock*, p. 76.

[43] Source: Krista Quiner, *Dominique Moceanu: A Gymnastics Sensation*, pp. 173, 177.

[44] Source: Herma Silverstein, *Mary Lou Retton and the New Gymnasts*, p. 15.

[45] Source: Steve Greenberg and Dale Ratermann, *I Remember Woody: Recollections of the Man They Called Coach Hayes*, pp. 149-150.

[46] Source: R.S. Ashby, *Sarah Hughes: America's Sweetheart*, p. 38.

[47] Source: Glen Macnow, *Sports Great Cal Ripken, Jr.*, pp. 16, 18.

[48] Source: Steve Greenberg and Dale Ratermann, *I Remember Woody: Recollections of the Man They Called Coach Hayes*, p. 36.

[49] Source: Herman L. Masin, *For Laughing Out Loud: Football's Funniest Stories*, p. 56.

[50] Source: Bart Rockwell, *World's Strangest Football Stories*, p. 62.

[51] Source: James A. Riley, *The Negro Leagues*, pp. 75-77.

[52] Source: Kurt Thomas and Kent Hannon, *Kurt Thomas on Gymnastics*, p. 81.

[53] Source: Marilyn Olsen, *Women Who Risk: Profiles of Women in Extreme Sports*, p. 45.

[54] Source: Jeff Savage, *Julie Krone: Unstoppable Jockey*, p. 38.

[55] Source: Hal Straus, editor, *Gymnastics Guide*, p. 346.

[56] Source: Jeff Savage, *Julie Foudy: Soccer Superstar*, p. 46.

[57] Source: Shiobhan Donohue, *Kristi Yamaguchi: Artist on Ice*, p. 45.

[58] Source: Norman L. Macht, *Babe Ruth*, pp. 29-30.

[59] Source: Herman L. Masin, *The Funniest Moments in Sports*, pp. 65-66.

[60] Source: Mac Davis, *Strange and Incredible Sports Happenings*, pp. 30-31.

[61] Source: Chris Crutcher, *King of the Mild Frontier*, p. 236.

[62] Source: Glen Macnow, *Sports Great Alex Rodriguez*, p. 42.

[63] Source: Mark Sufrin, *Payton*, p. 52.

[64] Source: "Fame Academy." *The Guardian*. 13 September 2008 <http://www.guardian.co.uk/lifeandstyle/2008/sep/13/celebrity.television>.

[65] Source: Michael J. Rosen, editor, *Dog People: Writers and Artists on Canine Companionship*, p. 59.

[66] Source: Elfi Schlegel and Claire Ross Dunn, *The Gymnastics Book*, p. 101.

[67] Source: Bill Gutman, *More Modern Women Superstars*, pp. 69-70.

[68] Source: Dave Kindred, *Heroes, Fools, and Other Dreamers*, p. 217.

[69] Source: Thomas W. Gilbert, *Roberto Clemente*, pp. 29-30.

[70] Source: Bill Gutman, *More Modern Women Superstars*, pp. 14-15.

[71] Source: Hal Straus, editor, *Gymnastics Guide*, pp. 318-319.

[72] Source: Septima Green, *Top 10 Women Gymnasts*, p. 8.

[73] Source: Paul Steenkamer, *Sports Great Donovan McNabb*, pp. 27-28, 30, 60.

[74] Source: Jerry Clower, *Let the Hammer Down!*, pp. 177-179.

[75] Source: Nathan Aaseng, *Sports Great John Stockton*, pp. 9, 17.

[76] Source: James Haskins, *Babe Ruth and Hank Aaron: The Home Run Kings*, p. 105.

[77] Source: Louise A. Gikow, *Extreme Sports*, pp. 32, 34.

[78] Source: Paul Greenberg, *Resonant Lives: 60 Figures of Consequence*, p. 101.

[79] Source: Chuck King, *The Funniest Thing I've Ever Seen*, pp. 81-82.

[80] Source: Shepard Long, *Carl Yastrzemski*, pp. 30-31.

[81] Source: Jeanne Marie Laskas, *We Remember*, p. 32.

[82] Source: Herman L. Masin, *For Laughing Out Loud: Football's Funniest Stories*, p. 50.

[83] Source: Shepard Long, *Carl Yastrzemski*, pp. 16-19, 22-23.

[84] Source: Bill Russell, *Red and Me: My Coach, My Lifelong Friend*, pp. 15-16.

[85] Source: Nathan Aaseng, *Sports Great David Robinson*, pp. 14-15.

[86] Source: Chris Crutcher, *King of the Mild Frontier*, p. 238.

[87] Source: Terri Morgan, *Gabrielle Reece: Volleyball's Model Athlete*, p. 17.

[88] Source: Bart Rockwell, *World's Strangest Hockey Stories*, p. 63.

[89] Source: Jim Campbell, *The Importance of Joe Louis*, p. 43.

[90] Source: Jacob Margolies, *The Negro Leagues: The Story of Black Baseball*, p. 34.

[91] Source: Robert Gardner and Dennis Shortelle, *The Forgotten Players: The Story of Black Baseball in America*, pp. 80-81.

[92] Source: Nadia Comaneci, *Letters to a Young Gymnast*, p. 108.

[93] Source: Jim Murray, *The Best of Jim Murray*, pp. 167-168.

[94] Source: Robert Lipsyte, *Assignment: Sports*, pp. 87-88.

[95] Source: Bela Karolyi and Nancy Ann Richardson, *Feel No Fear*, p. 12.

[96] Source: Lynn Haney, *Perfect Balance*, pp. 52-53.

[97] Source: Paul Steenkamer, *Sports Great Donovan McNabb*, pp. 13, 18.

[98] Source: Msgr. Vincent Fecher, *"The Lord and I": Vignettes from the Life of a Parish Priest*, pp. 57-58.

[99] Source: Ron Knapp, *Sports Great Bo Jackson*, p. 13.

[100] Source: Don L. Wulffson, *When Human Heads Were Footballs*, pp. 1-2.

[101] Source: Jimmy Crum and Carole Gerber, *How About That!*, pp. 25-26.

[102] Source: Jane Gottesman, *Game Face: What Does A Female Athlete Look Like?*, pp. 76-77.

[103] Source: Chris Lemmon, *A Twist of Lemmon: A Tribute to My Father*, pp. 113-116.

[104] Source: Barbara Long, *Jim Thorpe: Legendary Athlete*, pp. 78-79.

[105] Source: Howard Bragman, "Paper Trail: How to Come Out." *The Advocate.* 20 January 2009 <http://www.advocate.com/exclusive_detail_ektid70585.asp>.

[106] Source: John Albert Torres and Michael John Sullivan, *Sports Great Darryl Strawberry*, pp. 50-51.

[107] Source: Arthur Marx, *Son of Groucho*, p. 49.

[108] Source: Jimmy Crum and Carole Gerber, *How About That!*, p. 181.

[109] Source: Jane Gottesman, *Game Face: What Does A Female Athlete Look Like?*, p. 207.

[110] Source: Chris Lemmon, *A Twist of Lemmon: A Tribute to My Father*, p. 99.

[111] Source: Laurie Lindop, *Athletes*, pp. 37-38, 45.

[112] Source: Rob Wood, editor, *It's All in the Game: Funny Happenings for Those Who Love Sports*, p. 12.

[113] Source: Eric Silver, *The Book of the Just: The Unsung Heroes Who Rescued Jews from Hitler*, pp. 154-156. Also: "Max Schmeling: The Story of a Hero." <http://www.auschwitz.dk/schmeling.htm>.

[114] Source: Norman L. Macht, *Babe Ruth*, pp. 19, 40, 51.

[115] Source: Jim Murray, *The Best of Jim Murray*, p. 49.

[116] Source: Jack Kavanagh, *Sports Great Larry Bird*, p. 41.

[117] Source: Robert Lipsyte, *Assignment: Sports*, p. 12.

[118] Source: Jocko Conlan and Robert W. Creamer, *Jocko*, pp. 196-197.

[119] Source: John A. Torres, *Home-Run Hitters: Heroes of the Four Home-Run Game*, pp. 63-65.

[120] Source: Michael J. Pellowski, *Baseball's Funniest People*, p. 19.

[121] Source: Glen Macnow, *Sports Great Cal Ripken, Jr.*, p. 31.

[122] Source: James Haskins, *Babe Ruth and Hank Aaron: The Home Run Kings*, p. 43.

[123] Source: Ron Knapp, *Sports Great Bobby Bonilla*, p. 33.

[124] Source: Mac Davis, *100 Greatest Sports Feats*, p. 20.

[125] Source: Roger Ebert, "The best damn job in the whole damn world." 3 April 2009 <http://blogs.suntimes.com/ebert/2009/04/the_best_job_in_the_world.html>.

[126]Source: Bart Rockwell, *World's Strangest Hockey Stories*, p. 78.

[127]Source: Ron Knapp, *Sports Great Bo Jackson*, pp. 9, 44.

[128]Source: Donald J. Sobol, *Encyclopedia Brown's Book of the Wacky Outdoors*, p. 69.

[129] Source: Bill Deane, *Bob Gibson*, pp. 13, 16.

[130]Source: Sasha Cohen, *Fire on Ice*, pp. 33-34.

[131]Source: Denis J. Harrington, *Top 10 Women's Tennis Players*, pp. 6-9.

[132]Source: Morgan E. Hughes, *Mario Lemieux: Beating the Odds*, pp. 7, 10.

[133]Source: Donald J. Sobol, *Encyclopedia Brown's Book of Wacky Sports*, p. 89.

[134]Source: Chip Lovitt, *American Gymnasts: Gold Medal Dreams*, p. 76.

[135]Source: Fred Russell, teller, *Funny Thing About Sports*, p. 43.

[136]Source: Kermit Schafer, *Best of Bloopers*, p. 66.

[137]Source: Jerry Clower, *Ain't God Good!*, p. 30.

[138]Source: Herma Silverstein, *Mary Lou Retton and the New Gymnasts*, p. 65.

[139] Source: Michael J. Rosen, editor, *Dog People: Writers and Artists on Canine Companionship*, pp. 60-61.

[140] Source: Christopher Farran, *Dogs on the Job! True Stories of Phenomenal Dogs*, pp. 34-39.

[141] Source: Roger Ebert, "Perform a concert in words." *Chicago Sun-Times*. 8 December 2008 <http://blogs.suntimes.com/ebert/2008/12/perform_a_concert_in_words.html>.

[142] Source: James Haskins, *Sports Great Magic Johnson*, pp. 63-64.

[143] Source: Gary Cartwright, "Game over." *Texas Monthly*. June 2009 <http://www.texasmonthly.com/2009-06-01/cartwright-1.php>.

[144]Source: H. Allen Smith, *The Compleat Practical Joker*, pp. 136-137.

[145]Source: Ken Rappoport and Barry Wilner, *Girls Rule!*, p. 78.

[146] Source: Sam Molen, *They Make Me Laugh*, p. 43.

[147] Source: Gene Schoor, *Football's Greatest Coach: Vince Lombardi*, pp. 68-69.

[148] Source: Laurie Lindop, *Athletes*, p. 81.

[149] Source: Mike Towle, *I Remember Walter Payton*, p. 87.

[150]Source: Bela Karolyi and Nancy Ann Richardson, *Feel No Fear*, pp. 29-30.

[151] Source: Bill Barich, *The Sporting Life*, p. 23.

[152]Source: H. Allen Smith, *How to Write Without Knowing Nothing*, p. 42.

[153]Source: Art Linkletter, *I Wish I'd Said That!*, p. 51.

[154]Source: Toller Cranston, *Zero Tollerance*, pp. 45-46.

[155]Source: Ross R. Olney, *Lyn St. James: Driven to Be First*, p. 20.

[156] Source: Filip Bondy, "107 wins and counting for finals-bound Misty May-Treanor, Kerri Walsh." New York *Daily News*. 19 August 2008 <http://www.nydailynews.com/sports/2008olympics/2008/08/18/ 2008-08-18_107_wins_and_counting_for_finalsbound_mi.html>.

[157]Source: Kermit Schafer, *Best of Bloopers*, p. 62.

[158] Source: Steve Jacobson, *Carrying Jackie's Torch*, pp. 65, 67, 71, 73.

[159] Source: Stew Thornley, *Sports Great Greg Maddux*, p. 23.

[160] Source: Mac Davis, *Strange and Incredible Sports Happenings*, pp. 37-38.

[161]Source: Carl Erskine, *Carl Erskine's Tales from the Dodger Dugout*, p. 11.

[162] Source: Ron Knapp, *Sports Great Bobby Bonilla*, pp. 26, 33.

[163] Source: Larry Bortstein, *After Olympic Glory*, pp. 58-59.

[164]Source: Shiobhan Donohue, *Kristi Yamaguchi: Artist on Ice*, pp. 47-48.

[165]Source: Terri Morgan, *Gabrielle Reece: Volleyball's Model Athlete*, pp. 28, 31.

[166] Source: Thomas W. Gilbert, *Roberto Clemente*, p. 55.

[167] Source: Ken Rappoport and Barry Wilner, *Villains: The Bad Boys and Girls of Sport*, p. 140.

[168] Source: Bill Russell, *Red and Me: My Coach, My Lifelong Friend*, pp. 9-10.

[169]Source: Bill Gutman, *Tara Lipinski: Queen of the Ice*, p. 7.

[170]Source: Barbara Long, *Jim Thorpe: Legendary Athlete*, pp. 94-97.

[171]Source: Keith Elliot Greenberg, *Pro Wrestling: From Carnivals to Cable TV*, p. 107.

[172]Source: Harry "Steamboat" Johnson, *Standing the Gaff*, pp. 84-85.

[173]Source: Ross R. Olney, *Lyn St. James: Driven to Be First*, p. 23.

[174] Source: Jim Campbell, *The Importance of Joe Louis*, p. 77.

[175]Source: Ken Rappoport and Barry Wilner, *Girls Rule!*, p. 88.

[176]Source: Kathy Katella-Cofrancesco, *Economic Causes*, p. 28.

[177] Source: Joe Layden, *Kobe: The Story of the NBA's Rising Young Star*, pp. 36, 75.

[178]Source: Morgan E. Hughes, *Mario Lemieux: Beating the Odds*, p. 18.

[179] Source: Mary Packard, *Against the Odds: A Chapter Book*, pp. 24-33.

[180]Source: Joe Garner, *Stay Tuned: Television's Unforgettable Moments*, pp. 166-168.

[181] Source: Bud Greenspan, *100 Greatest Moments in Olympic History*, pp. 192-193.

[182] Source: Louise A. Gikow, *Extreme Sports*, pp. 29-30, 48.

[183]Source: Elfi Schlegel and Claire Ross Dunn, *The Gymnastics Book*, p. 112.

[184] Source: Carin T. Ford, *Muhammad Ali: "I Am the Greatest,"* p. 26.

[185]Source: Bill Gutman, *Tara Lipinski: Queen of the Ice*, pp. 25-26, 30.

[186]Source: Sasha Cohen, *Fire on Ice*, pp. 85-86.

[187]Source: Dan Gutman, *Gymnastics: The Trials, the Triumphs, the Truth*, p. 34.

[188]Source: Ron Jenkins, *Acrobats of the Soul*, p. 54.

[189] Source: Carl Erskine, *Carl Erskine's Tales from the Dodger Dugout*, pp. 27-28.

[190]Source: Michael J. Pellowski, *Baseball's Funniest People*, p. 31.

[191]Source: Joel Cohen, *Odd Moments in Baseball*, p. 67.

[192] Source: Elson Smith, *The Blooper Man*, p. 57.

[193] Source: Mac Davis, *100 Greatest Sports Feats*, p. 27.

[194] Source: Sam Molen, *Take 2 and Hit to Right*, pp. 102-103.

[195]Source: H. Allen Smith, *How to Write Without Knowing Nothing*, p. 41.

[196] Source: James A. Riley, *The Negro Leagues*, p. 59.

[197]Source: Herman L. Masin, *The Funniest Moments in Sports*, p. 21.

[198] Source: Chuck King, *The Funniest Thing I've Ever Seen*, pp. 93-95.

[199]Source: Fred Russell, *I'll Go Quietly*, p. 21.

[200]Source: Dave Kindred, *Heroes, Fools, and Other Dreamers*, pp. 83-85. Also see <http://www.baseballreliquary.org/Bresnahan.htm>.

[201] Source: Morris Eckhouse, *Bob Feller*, pp. 10, 42-43.

[202] Source: Elson Smith, *The Blooper Man*, pp. 32-33.

[203]Source: Kurt Thomas and Kent Hannon, *Kurt Thomas on Gymnastics*, pp. 153, 175.

[204] Source: William W. Lace, *Sports Great Nolan Ryan*, p. 34.

[205]Source: Bart Rockwell, *World's Strangest Hockey Stories*, p. 31.

[206]Source: Don Wade, *"And Then Arnie Told Chi Chi...,"* p. 195.

[207] Source: Carin T. Ford, *Muhammad Ali: "I Am the Greatest,"* p. 30-31.

[208]Source: Lynn Haney, *The Lady is a Jock*, p. 89.

[209]Source: Kathleen Krull, *Lives of the Athletes*, p. 69.

[210]Source: Bart Rockwell, *World's Strangest Football Stories*, p. 31.

[211] Source: Steve Jacobson, *Carrying Jackie's Torch*, pp. 47-48.

[212]Source: Sandra Bezic, *The Passion to Skate*, pp. 76, 81.

[213] Source: Christopher Farran, *Dogs on the Job! True Stories of Phenomenal Dogs*, pp. 1-6.

[214] Source: Tom Danehy, "Tom encourages you to get out and enjoy the games we Tucsonans play." *Tucson Weekly*. 25 September 2008 <http://www.tucsonweekly.com/gbase/Opinion/Content?oid=oid:115848>.

[215] Source: Sam Molen, *They Make Me Laugh*, pp. 56-57.

[216] Source: Stan W. Carlson, *Baseball Banter*, p. 8.

[217] Source: Tom Danehy, "Soccer sends kids like Brianna Caceres to college, so it can't be all bad." *Tucson Weekly*. 9 October 2008 <http://www.tucsonweekly.com/gbase/Opinion/Content?oid=oid:116771.>.

[218] Source: Nathan Aaseng, *Sports Great John Stockton*, pp. 46, 48.

[219]Source: Peggy Fleming, *The Long Program*, pp. 92-93.

[220] Source: Glenn Dickey, *Sports Great Kevin Mitchell*, pp. 13, 24, 31.

[221]Source: Don Wade, *"And Then Arnie Told Chi Chi...,"* p. 72.

[222]Source: Don L. Wulffson, *When Human Heads Were Footballs*, pp. 51-52.

[223] Source: Mark Edmundson, "Enough Already: What I'd really like to tell the bores in my life." *The American Scholar*. Summer 2009 <http://www.theamericanscholar.org/enough-already/>.

[224]Source: Sandra Bezic, *The Passion to Skate*, p. 69.

[225] Source: S. Claus, *Holiday Cheer for the 19th Hole*, p. 25.

[226]Source: Mark Sufrin, *Payton*, p. 7.

[227]Source: Kathleen Krull, *Lives of the Athletes*, pp. 34-35.

[228]Source: H. Allen Smith, *The Compleat Practical Joker*, pp. 295-296.

[229] Source: Sam Molen, *Take 2 and Hit to Right*, p. 85.

[230] Source: Bill Deane, *Bob Gibson*, pp. 26, 29-30, 48. Also: "Bob Gibson." Accessed 9 January 2010 <http://www.baseballlibrary.com/ballplayers/player.php?name=Bob_Gibson_1935.>

[231]Source: Mike Towle, *I Remember Arthur Ashe*, pp. 67-68.

[232] Source: S. Claus, *Holiday Cheer for the 19th Hole*, p. 19.

[233]Source: Joel Cohen, *Odd Moments in Baseball*, p. 42.

[234]Source: R.S. Ashby, *Sarah Hughes: America's Sweetheart*, pp. 58-59.

[235] Source: Jim Benagh, *Sports Great Herschel Walker*, pp. 16-20, 25.

[236]Source: Marilyn Olsen, *Women Who Risk: Profiles of Women in Extreme Sports*, p. 54.

[237] Source: Stan W. Carlson, *Baseball Banter*, pp. 3-4.

[238]Source: Harry "Steamboat" Johnson, *Standing the Gaff*, p. 113.

[239]Source: Joe Garagiola, *It's Anybody's Ballgame*, p. 62.

[240]Source: John C. Skipper, *Umpires*, p. 56.

[241]Source: S.H. Burchard, *Pelé*, pp. 7-8, 11, 28.

[242]Source: Art Linkletter, *I Wish I'd Said That!*, p. 17.

[243]Source: Mike Towle, *I Remember Arthur Ashe*, pp. 143-144.

[244]Source: Jocko Conlan and Robert W. Creamer, *Jocko*, p. 84.

[245] Source: Gene Schoor, *Football's Greatest Coach: Vince Lombardi*, pp. 172-174.

[246] Source: Glen Macnow, *Sports Great Alex Rodriguez*, pp. 34-35.

[247]Source: John C. Skipper, *Umpires*, p. 133.

[248] Source: Larry Bortstein, *After Olympic Glory*, pp. 47, 49.

[249] Source: Stew Thornley, *Sports Great Greg Maddux*, pp. 48-51, 58, 60.

[250] Source: John A. Torres, *Home-Run Hitters: Heroes of the Four Home-Run Game*, pp. 45-46.